BIBLE

CUES & CLUES

101 WORD SEARCH PUZZLES
TEST YOUR

BIBLE KNOWLEDGE

BARBOUR BOOKS
An Imprint of Barbour Publishing, Inc.

Print ISBN 978-1-68322-121-0

Compiled by Brigitta Nortker and Sara Stoker.

Published by Barbour Books, an imprint of Barbour Publishing, Inc., P.O. Box 719, Uhrichsville, Ohio 44683, www.barbourbooks.com

Our mission is to publish and distribute inspirational products offering exceptional value and biblical encouragement to the masses.

Member of the
Evangelical Christian
Publishers Association

Printed in the United States of America.

BIBLE CUES AND CLUES

Introducing a brand-new Bible word search game. . .with a twist!

Each of the 101 word search puzzles features Bible clues given in the form of trivia. Figure out the correct answers to the Bible trivia in order to discover the words you need to search for in the puzzle grid. Scripture hints are provided in case you need help along the way.

Bible Cues and Clues: 101 Word Search Puzzles Test Your Bible Knowledge is a fun way to learn more about God's Word!

Puzzle 1

1. Who called Jesus the Lamb of God? (John 1:29)
2. Fill in the blank: Paul says that the Law was our _____ to bring us to Christ. (Galatians 3:24 NKJV)
3. Fill in the blank: The waters returned and covered the host of Pharaoh and there remained "not so much as _____ of them." (Exodus 14:28)
4. On what mountain was Moses on when he saw the burning bush? (Exodus 3:1)
5. How many mites did the poor widow put in the temple treasury? (Mark 12:42)
6. Moses fled Egypt because he did what to an Egyptian for smiting a Hebrew? (Exodus 2:11–15 NKJV)
7. What name means "God with us"? (Matthew 1:23)
8. Where did God tell Joseph to take Mary and Jesus to keep them safe? (Matthew 2:13)
9. In Nebuchadnezzar's dream, the image's chest and arms were made out of what material? (Daniel 2:32)
10. What was Luke's occupation? (Colossians 4:14)
11. John said that what can overcome the world? (1 John 5:4)
12. Which missionary companion had a godly Jewish mother and a Greek father? (Acts 16:1 NKJV)
13. On what site did Solomon build the temple? (2 Chronicles 3:1)
14. What high priest in King Josiah's reign discovered the Book of the Law while repairing the temple? (2 Kings 22:8)
15. What object of the children's are set on edge? (Ezekiel 18:2)
16. What was the name of the gate that the sons of Hassenaah built? (Nehemiah 3:3)
17. How were Esther and Mordecai related? (Esther 2:7)
18. David said he never saw the righteous be what? (Psalm 37:25)

19. What church worshiped on the first day of the week and brought offerings for the suffering saints in Judea? (1 Corinthians 16:1–2)
20. What edible substance did Samson find in the carcass of the lion he killed earlier? (Judges 14:8)

```
W P N A B T P Y E G G T T I N
M N H U P A V Y H T O M I T O
F U N Y S E E H O R E B S A C
I A G E S K S T N Z O I T W O
A E I O U I G T E E T H I H U
H F C A L C K Y P O I J U S
T W A W H L E I A P T L I C I
O A W I M E Y B A N K K B O N
T X T Q T D E P O N Y I B I S
V R U U L H E L E U N A M M E
X Y L A T M E P E O P H O A X
J I E N T O N E S D D R I V L
S H H L E U R Q N S I L V E R
F O R S A K E N M A F T R E S
J M I A S E K T H T N I R O C
```

PUZZLE 2

1. Fill in the blank: Paul wrote that we are to bring into captivity every thought to the _____ of Christ. (2 Corinthians 10:5)

2. What was the name of the idol that kept falling on its face in front of the ark of the covenant? (1 Samuel 5:3)

3. Which disciple brought the boy with the five loaves and two fish to Jesus? (John 6:8-9)

4. Besides the red, black, and pale colored horses, what was the color of the other horse mentioned in Revelation 6? (Revelation 6:2)

5. Fill in the blank: Each of the living creatures had faces of a human being, a lion, an ox, and an _____ . (Ezekiel 1:10)

6. What king in Daniel's time decided to drink wine from the vessels taken from the temple of Jerusalem? (Daniel 5:2)

7. Fill in the blank: Passover is also known as the Feast of _____ Bread. (Exodus 23:15)

8. When the Israelites camped in the wilderness, on what side of the tabernacle did the tribes of Judah, Zebulun, and Issachar camp together? (Numbers 2:3-9)

9. Isaiah 55:12 says all the trees of the field will do what with their hands? (Isaiah 55:12)

10. Fill in the blank: "And Jesus said unto him, Verily I say unto thee, _____ shalt thou be with me in paradise." (Luke 23:43)

11. Fill in the blank: "Thou shalt not bear _____ witness against thy neighbour." (Exodus 20:16)

12. Fill in the blank: The inside of the house of the Lord was overlaid with _____ . (1 Kings 6:21)

13. The four corners of the altar had what? (Exodus 27:2)

14. What does Paul say we do not do against flesh and blood? (Ephesians 6:12)

15. What was the name of the wilderness that Moses sent the twelve spies into the Promised Land from? (Numbers 13:3)

16. What prophet did God call "son of man"? (Ezekiel 33:1-2)

17. What did the Israelites sing a song to in the wilderness? (Numbers 21:16-17)

18. What did Jesus say we are slaves to? (John 8:34 NIV)

19. Besides the sun and the stars, what else did God create that He said would be for signs and seasons and days and years? (Genesis 1:14-16)

20. Besides goodness, what else did the psalmist say would follow him "all the days of my life"? (Psalm 23:6)

21. How many eunuchs did King Ahasuerus have waiting on him? (Esther 1:10 NIV)

22. Fill in the blank: "But I say unto you, _____ your enemies." (Matthew 5:44)

```
U  N  L  A  E  V  E  N  D  E  N  E  A  V  R
M  D  G  L  O  D  N  O  O  B  E  N  D  A  B
C  X  E  C  N  E  I  D  E  B  O  P  A  B  F
L  Q  A  N  D  R  E  W  N  O  U  H  G  A  N
S  F  I  M  E  B  V  H  M  A  N  E  O  S  I
A  L  A  U  Y  V  C  A  S  E  V  E  N  Y  C
F  B  E  L  S  H  A  Z  Z  A  R  R  J  U  E
E  A  W  Q  S  M  P  E  O  N  O  C  B  A  T
T  Y  S  E  W  E  K  A  L  H  O  P  Y  J  O
I  I  Q  G  U  I  D  G  K  N  A  R  A  P  D
H  E  N  O  E  L  A  L  S  V  U  S  D  A  Y
W  E  L  L  B  E  L  E  S  P  U  N  O  B  A
N  V  O  D  P  H  F  S  A  X  I  B  T  C  B
L  I  V  A  R  E  E  L  T  S  E  R  W  A  C
K  U  E  V  M  D  C  X  I  S  T  W  A  R  D
```

Puzzle 3

1. Samson killed a lion with what kind of hands? (Judges 14:5–6 NIV)
2. According to Psalm 24:1, what object is the Lord's? (Psalm 24:1)
3. Ahab and who else joined together to become a wicked pair who took issue with the prophecies of Elijah? (1 Kings 19:1–2)
4. Besides Jesus, who else raised someone from the dead in the New Testament? (Acts 9:36–40)
5. Who was Jesus talking to when He asked "Are you not therefore mistaken, because you do not know the Scriptures?" (Mark 12:18, 24 NKJV)
6. When Queen Esther came unannounced to see King Xerxes, she would be killed unless the king did what with his scepter? (Esther 4:11 NIV)
7. Adam's punishment for disobeying God in the Garden of Eden mean banishment and to do what with the ground? (Genesis 3:23)
8. What book of the Bible comes right before Habakkuk? (Table of Contents)
9. What military tactic did Joshua use to finally take the small city? (Joshua 8:4 NIV)
10. What high priest said it was expedient that one man should die for the people? (John 11:49–50)
11. What goeth before destruction? (Proverbs 16:18)
12. Pharaoh's magicians duplicated three of the plagues: water to blood, frogs, and what object was turned into a snake? (Exodus 7:12)
13. What type of blossoms were the holders on the lampstand in the tabernacle designed to look like? (Exodus 37:20)
14. When Jesus preached, "Woe unto you, scribes and Pharisees, hypocrites!," what animal was swallowed to illustrate His point? (Matthew 23:23–24)

15. Fill in the bank: "The disciples were called Christians first in _____ ." (Acts 11:26)

16. After Paul's arrest in Jerusalem, the centurion hesitated to flog Paul because he was what type of citizen? (Acts 22:25)

17. In Revelation 2:17, the church at Pergamos was told that if they overcame, they would be given what type of manna? (Revelation 2:17)

18. What was Pontius Pilate's job? (Luke 3:1)

19. What did Joseph make the children of Israel swear an oath to carry out of Egypt? (Genesis 50:25)

20. In Nebuchadnezzar's dream image, the image's legs were made of clay and what other material? (Daniel 2:33)

21. Who was Caesar at the time Jesus was born? (Luke 2:1)

22. On what part of His hands does God say He has inscribed our names? (Isaiah 49:16)

```
A U G U A S T U S B O N P I P
X N A M O R G O V S T A R N M
K O L B C D S E R E L L I T U
H J M R A E A F A M J P D L M
I U O Y N R T E S W E Q E H A
B D N E T X E M O O Z T S I V
L A D H I D D E N O E U S Z U
X E L E O D S W A C B E V R T
J H M T C H C O I M E B R O M
W A S A H P A I A C L T Y N X
U Y T R C N S T U N T K A R E
T O I Y L S A D N S R E T E P
G U R O D P D H Z I H F A V W
E R O T Y A U G U S T U S O G
B O N E S J E Z A M B E V G C
```

Puzzle 4

1. The Garden of Gethsemane was on the Mount of what? (Luke 22:39)

2. The exiles in Babylon mourned the loss of what city? (Lamentations 1:1–9)

3. Which of the following instruments is not mentioned in the Bible; tambourine, lute, trumpet, or trombone? (1 Samuel 18:6; Psalm 92:3; Joshua 6:4)

4. Who was Timothy's mother? (2 Timothy 1:5)

5. What of the potter's was bought with the thirty pieces of silver after Judas threw them back at the Pharisees? (Matthew 27:7)

6. Jesus' first recorded miracle was at Cana of Galilee when He turned what into wine? (John 2:9)

7. When Jesus prophesied about His death, which minor prophet did He say was a sign? (Matthew 12:39–40 NIV)

8. Fill in the blank: Revelation 5:5 calls Jesus the _____ of the tribe of Judah. (Revelation 5:5)

9. Which of the seven churches in Revelation was told they would have hidden manna to eat? (Revelation 2:12, 17)

10. What will burn with fire and brimstone that Revelation 21:8 says that all liars will have their part in? (Revelation 21:8)

11. How many times does Lucifer say "I will"? (Isaiah 14:13–14)

12. Who was Abraham's second wife? (Genesis 25:1)

13. Fill in the blank: John said if we walk in the light as Jesus is in the light, we have _____ with each other. (1 John 1:7)

14. What otherwise good king was stricken with leprosy for burning incense in the temple? (2 Chronicles 26:19)

15. Fill in the blank: The Lord told Moses to _____ all the firstborn. (Exodus 13:2)

16. The supper of the Lamb in heaven celebrates what occasion? (Revelation 19:9)

17. Fill in the blank: Jesus said not a jot or _____ will pass away from the Law until it is fulfilled. (Matthew 5:18)

18. Who said, "To obey is better than sacrifice," to King Saul? (1 Samuel 15:22)

19. What type of plant was to be dipped in the blood to put the blood on the doorposts? (Exodus 12:22)

20. Fill in the blank: As Paul spoke of the judgment to come, Felix became fearful and said, "You may leave. When I find it _____, I will send for you." (Acts 24:25 NIV)

21. How many days passed between the first and second plagues? (Exodus 7:25)

22. What were Peter, James, and John doing while Jesus was praying and agonizing in Gethsemane? (Matthew 26:36–40)

```
T D A F K E T U R A H S B O F
R E W E K X I Y O J M L I K E
O Q Z A V E F B B D L E I F L
B U L O L I V E S M N E P N S
M Z N T T G F J S A M P O I O
O Z T C H Y S S O P E I Y H M
N I N E T W E R U N L N Y T A
T A C O R M A R R I A G E U G
S H R V O N Y T H K S H L A R
A B A X M E Q Z E E U N I C E
M V H P B V M F V R R F R E P
U E U C O N V E N I E N T E D
E A T B N P N M B R J R H C L
L X E F E L L O W S H I P E I
Z D K A E T B V Q W P S H M F
```

PUZZLE 5

1. What was Paul's "heart's desire and prayer to God" for Israel's people? (Romans 10:1)

2. What does the Lord prepare for us in the presence of our enemies? (Psalm 23:5)

3. What was the short outer garment priests wore over their robes? (Exodus 28:6-8)

4. What priest had sons named Hophni and Phinehas? (1 Samuel 4:16-17)

5. What part of the priests had to touch the water before the Jordan River began to go dry? (Joshua 3:15-16)

6. Besides Elijah, what prophet did Ahab complain always prophesied against him? (1 Kings 22:17-18 NIV)

7. According to Mosaic law, what was the punishment for one who blasphemed God's name? (Leviticus 24:16)

8. After Esther agreed to speak to the king, she told Mordecai to tell the people to fast for how many days? (Esther 4:16)

9. Who was Jesus talking to when He asked "Why do you think evil in your hearts"? (Matthew 9:3-4 NKJV)

10. Who said this: "I cast it into the fire, and this calf came out"? (Exodus 32:22-24 NKJV)

11. A dead man came back to life because his body fell on the bones of what prophet? (2 Kings 13:21)

12. What was the name of the gate Hanun and the inhabitants of Zanoah repaired? (Nehemiah 3:13)

13. Who was married to Elimelech and had sons named Mahlon and Chilion? (Ruth 1:2)

14. According to Mark, where did Jesus often teach in Nazareth on the Sabbath? (Mark 6:2)

15. Fill in the blank: "Nor is there salvation in any other, for there is no other _____ under heaven given among men by which we must be saved." (Acts 4:12 NKJV)

16. When enemies tried to kill Samson in Gaza, he carried away what part of the city fixture? (Judges 16:2–3)

17. What group of Pharaoh's people drowned in the Red Sea? (Exodus 14:28)

18. Jesus came to do what with the Law and the Prophets? (Matthew 5:17)

19. What plant of the field did Jesus say was arrayed with greater splendor than Solomon? (Matthew 6:28–29)

20. When the sheep is found, the shepherd rejoices and lays it on what? (Luke 15:5)

21. How do the rod and the staff help the psalmist "fear no evil" in spite of walking in the "shadow of death"? (Psalm 23:4)

22. Fill in the blank: Paul told the Galatians that we are no longer slaves but _____ . (Galatians 4:7 NKJV)

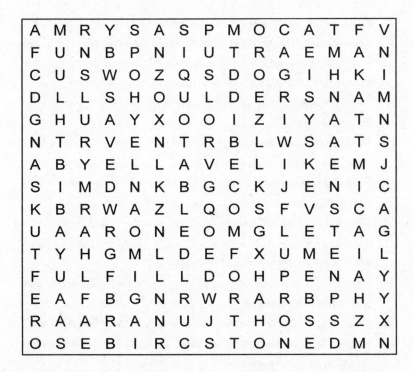

```
A M R Y S A S P M O C A T F V
F U N B P N I U T R A E M A N
C U S W O Z Q S D O G I H K I
D L L S H O U L D E R S N A M
G H U A Y X O O I Z I Y A T N
N T R V E N T R B L W S A T S
A B Y E L L A V E L I K E M J
S I M D N K B G C K J E N I C
K B R W A Z L Q O S F V S C A
U A A R O N E O M G L E T A G
T Y H G M L D E F X U M E I L
F U L F I L L D O H P E N A Y
E A F B G N R W R A R B P H Y
R A A R A N U J T H O S S Z X
O S E B I R C S T O N E D M N
```

Puzzle 6

1. When Pharaoh's magicians turned their rods into serpents, what did Aaron's snake do to theirs? (Exodus 7:12)

2. In the song the women sang that made King Saul even more jealous of David, how many did they sing that King Saul had slain? (1 Samuel 18:7)

3. Absalom, David's son, led a rebellion against his father and was finally captured and killed because what of his got caught in a tree? (2 Samuel 14:26; 18:9)

4. Which son kept his brothers from killing Joseph and instead threw Joseph into a pit? (Genesis 37:21–22)

5. In what part of the house did Rahab hide the spies? (Joshua 2:6)

6. Fill in the blank: Paul says we are more than ___ through Him who loved us. (Romans 8:37)

7. When Jacob was blessing his sons, which son's blessing contained a reference to the Stone of Israel? (Genesis 49:22–24)

8. How many days did the people celebrate following the completion of Solomon's temple? (1 Kings 8:65)

9. Fill in the blank: "Thou shalt not make unto thee any ___ image." (Exodus 20:4)

10. To which church in Revelation does Jesus say He will come upon them as a thief? (Revelation 3:1–3)

11. Fill in the blank: When Jesus was transfigured, His face shone like the ___. (Matthew 17:2)

12. What kind of tree did Zacchaeus climb in order to see Jesus? (Luke 19:4)

13. What tribe was Moses from? (Exodus 2:1)

14. What word, which was difficult to pronounce, was used to trap the Ephraimites? (Judges 12:4–6)

15. Solomon told his son to apply what to understanding? (Proverbs 2:2)

16. Besides "that old serpent" and "devil," what other description of Satan appears in Revelation 12:9? (Revelation 12:9)

17. What was the name of the valley that Delilah from the Old Testament lived in? (Judges 16:4)
18. What was the scroll doing in Zechariah's vision? (Zechariah 5:1)
19. When he was a boy, what was David's weapon of choice? (1 Samuel 17:40)
20. What name means "the glory has departed"? (1 Samuel 4:21)
21. Who was born looking red? (Genesis 25:25)
22. The seven men chosen in Acts 6 were to serve whom among the Greeks and make sure they were provided for? (Acts 6:1, 3)

H	C	N	E	E	T	R	U	O	F	S	P	H	R	J
G	O	D	S	Q	Z	H	P	O	N	O	M	Y	O	A
G	N	I	Y	L	F	N	O	G	A	R	D	S	F	E
S	Q	F	C	D	S	R	H	A	P	E	E	I	U	K
C	U	V	A	H	G	U	T	I	W	K	O	D	A	W
X	E	N	M	U	A	S	E	O	V	U	Y	T	R	Q
D	R	T	O	J	G	B	L	P	H	F	R	R	E	S
X	O	Z	R	J	O	L	O	G	R	A	V	E	N	I
D	R	F	E	O	A	K	B	D	E	D	E	U	R	D
P	S	N	I	W	I	J	B	H	X	P	O	B	K	R
E	O	R	S	I	S	L	I	N	G	H	A	E	Z	A
C	I	M	V	D	C	T	H	O	U	S	A	N	D	S
H	P	E	S	O	J	Q	S	X	M	N	L	I	F	R
P	L	V	B	W	N	I	I	A	H	T	P	C	R	Z
W	Q	S	X	S	K	F	U	O	R	T	E	E	M	A

Puzzle 7

1. Who touched the ark of the covenant and died? (2 Samuel 6:6-7)

2. What type of birds did the Lord send for the Israelites to eat? (Exodus 16:13)

3. Fill in the blank: Ecclesiastes 9:16 says wisdom is better than _____ . (Ecclesiastes 9:16)

4. Fill in the blank: Satan was _____ by the blood of the Lamb. (Revelation 12:11)

5. Jesus came to do what to those under the Law? (Galatians 4:4-5)

6. Besides dancing, what else did the Israelites do immediately after the Lord brought His people out of Egypt? (Exodus 15:1, 21)

7. Who fought a battle with torches hidden in pitchers? (Judges 7:15-16)

8. According to Isaiah 11:7, what will the lion eat like the ox in the kingdom of God? (Isaiah 11:7)

9. Who was Jonathan's son? (2 Samuel 4:4)

10. Fill in the blank: A lying tongue is but for a _____ . (Proverbs 12:19)

11. How did the manna spoil if the Israelites left it overnight? (Exodus 16:20)

12. Of the seven churches in Revelation, which church was admonished for compromising their beliefs with worldly ideas? (Revelation 2:12-17)

13. What word is defined as "Oh Lord, come!"? (1 Corinthians 16:22)

14. Who stole treasure from the devastated city of Jericho and paid for his sin with his life? (Joshua 7:20-21)

15. Jesus said He is what and we are the branches? (John 15:1, 5)

16. The moneychangers had made the temple a den of thieves, but it should have been called what kind of house by all nations? (Mark 11:17)

17. What sea was parted as the people exited? (Exodus 13:18; 14:21, 31)

18. How many daughters did Hannah have? (1 Samuel 2:21)

19. What was the name of the mountain that God took Moses up when He showed Moses all of the Promised Land? (Deuteronomy 34:1-2)

20. Whose daughter did Jesus raise when He had the mourners removed so He could perform the miracle? (Mark 5:22, 36–42)

21. What title was used by the voice from heaven to describe Jesus' position as Son following his baptism? (Matthew 3:17)

22. Fill in the blank: Whosoever shall call upon the name of the Lord shall be _____ . (Romans 10:13)

```
V  I  M  E  V  A  Y  J  M  Q  M  E  N  T  A
Q  H  T  D  U  I  P  O  K  M  U  N  H  F  S
D  S  T  R  E  N  G  T  H  H  D  A  R  B  W
A  T  J  E  E  V  X  P  R  A  Z  R  I  E  A
W  R  A  B  H  P  A  Y  R  Z  R  E  O  L  I
E  N  I  V  B  S  P  S  U  S  E  Y  J  O  H
P  E  R  G  A  M  O  S  M  I  D  F  R  V  X
L  T  U  A  I  A  T  B  Z  P  E  W  Q  E  Z
I  H  S  S  U  R  V  G  I  D  E  O  N  D  D
A  C  H  N  A  A  T  S  K  H  M  Z  W  K  O
I  J  P  W  I  N  G  C  V  B  P  D  O  S  A
U  T  R  W  A  A  G  P  R  A  Y  E  R  R  K
Q  W  Z  H  H  T  K  T  N  E  M  O  M  O  I
E  R  C  Y  I  H  O  W  P  X  G  H  S  J  D
A  A  B  E  V  A  H  O  V  E  R  C  O  M  E
```

PUZZLE 8

1. Philippians 2:9 says that God gave Jesus the name that is what to every other name? (Philippians 2:9)

2. What was the first thing the angel said to the shepherds: "Do not be _____ "? (Luke 2:10 NIV)

3. What did Samson cut off and thereby break a Nazarite vow which caused his death? (Judges 16:17)

4. In Nebuchadnezzar's dream image, the image's belly and thighs were made of what material? (Daniel 2:32 NIV)

5. What word means "stone of help"? (1 Samuel 7:12)

6. What wife of King Herod engineered the execution of John the Baptist? (Matthew 14:6–8)

7. Fill in the blank: You shall not bear _____ witness against your neighbor. (Exodus 20:16)

8. What occupation did the woman from Endor have? (1 Samuel 28:7–8 NIV)

9. What did the centurion named Julius show toward Paul during the voyage to Rome? (Acts 27:1–3 NIV)

10. Who brought gifts from the Philippians to Paul while he was imprisoned in Rome? (Philippians 4:18)

11. What number day of the month was the Passover lamb to be killed? (Exodus 12:6)

12. What wind took the locusts away? (Exodus 10:19)

13. When Daniel first arrived in Babylon, what type of food did he immediately refuse to eat? (Daniel 1:8)

14. What substance was Lot's wife turned into when she looked back at the destruction of a wicked city? (Genesis 19:26)

15. Esther's husband, Ahasuerus (also known as Xerxes) ruled 127 provinces from India to what country? (Esther 1:1)

16. Who was stricken with leprosy because she spoke against her brother's wife? (Numbers 12:1, 10)

17. Fill in the blank: The psalmist said the Lord surrounds the righteous with _____ . (Psalm 5:12)

18. What are we to present to God as a living sacrifice? (Romans 12:1)

19. Jesus likens false prophets to what animal wearing sheep's clothing? (Matthew 7:15)

20. The Ethiopian eunuch in the book of Acts held what position? (Acts 8:27)

21. When Jacob worked for Laban, he agreed to take all of the spotted, brown, and what other kind of sheep as his pay? (Genesis 30:32)

22. Sin is a what to any people? (Proverbs 14:34)

```
S  P  E  C  K  L  E  D  A  W  E  Y  F  Z  X
R  W  T  R  E  T  Z  D  S  E  I  D  O  B  C
E  M  R  W  T  A  E  M  M  S  K  H  U  P  S
P  D  E  O  N  Z  O  S  V  T  A  C  R  U  I
R  F  A  L  S  E  R  W  S  S  A  L  T  X  J
A  L  S  V  A  I  B  H  S  A  O  I  E  M  U
O  K  U  E  E  R  C  E  E  D  D  W  E  M  I
C  C  R  S  V  A  L  A  N  O  V  L  N  A  S
F  E  E  Q  O  S  F  A  R  E  R  P  T  I  E
A  P  R  R  B  R  X  H  N  E  Z  N  O  R  B
V  S  P  D  A  I  P  O  I  H  T  E  F  I  M
O  E  R  I  T  A  U  I  K  O  P  R  R  M  K
R  X  D  B  P  H  E  R  O  D  I  A  S  N  D
F  S  S  E  N  D  N  I  K  B  A  M  W  S  X
U  N  C  L  E  A  E  N  N  M  U  I  D  E  M
```

Puzzle 9

1. When John first saw the Lamb in heaven, what was the Lamb doing? (Revelation 5:6)

2. What Bible word means "What is it?" (Exodus 16:15, 31)

3. What was Joshua's name before Moses called him Joshua? (Numbers 13:16 NIV)

4. King Xerxes (also known as Ahasuerus) ruled from Ethiopia to what country? (Esther 1:1)

5. What shouldn't you do frequently with your neighbor? (Proverbs 25:17)

6. Where did Lucifer fall from? (Isaiah 14:12)

7. What tribal background did King Saul come from? (1 Samuel 9:1-2)

8. John said there would be no more death, sorrow, or pain in heaven because what type of things will have passed away? (Revelation 21:4)

9. Before Jesus calmed the sea, what was He doing in the boat? (Mark 4:38)

10. What part of the chariots did the Lord remove when He troubled the hosts of Egypt? (Exodus 14:25)

11. Who wanted to change her name to Mara? (Ruth 1:20)

12. What did Elijah call down from heaven to defeat the prophets of Baal on Mount Carmel? (1 Kings 18:38)

13. On how many commandments did Jesus say all of the Law and the Prophets hang? (Matthew 22:40)

14. What did Jezebel get thrown out of which led to her death? (2 Kings 9:32-33)

15. Who was the king of Zidon, the father of Jezebel? (1 Kings 16:31)

16. In Nebuchadnezzar's dream image, what part of the image was made of gold? (Daniel 2:32)

17. What more familiar name now applies to the ancient city of Jebus? (Judges 19:10)

18. Fill in the blank: The psalmist says that in keeping God's law there is great _____ . (Psalm 19:11)

19. Fill in the blank: In Revelation 1:8, Jesus says He is the Alpha and the _____ , the beginning and the end. (Revelation 1:8)
20. Selah means a _____ or the end. (Psalm 3:8)
21. Who led a rebellion against Moses and Aaron in the wilderness? (Numbers 16:1-3)
22. Besides a pair of young pigeons, what other pair of animals is said in the Law to be appropriate for the sacrifice given for Jesus' presentation at the temple shortly after He was born? (Luke 2:24)

```
W R I N D K B E N J A N I M E
I E T H B A A L K Z V X D R R
N W B N O A M I G F T I S O A
L A A H C T E E N I M S S F Z
O R G A W O D N I W L J F I Q
V D A E H A S H P E D G N R T
I G W R M T P O E R L D I E Y
S X J O H O S H E A I L M P K
I R Y Q C V W B L A V S A A O
V E P A M E L A S U R E J B R
I S T A N D I N G Z P K N N A
M X N T U R T L E D O V E S U
O N Z S A S R U I W P K B X H
A E F O R M E R T A U K M N Z
N I T U R T L E D O H A R O K
```

Puzzle 10

1. How many loaves of bread were used when Jesus fed the 4,000? (Matthew 15:34)

2. What were Peter and Andrew casting their nets into when Jesus called them to follow Him? (Matthew 4:18)

3. What queen refused to join the king's feast so he could show her beauty to everyone present? (Esther 1:12)

4. What does Sheol mean? (Psalm 16:10)

5. Who was the king of Assyria during Hezekiah's reign? (2 Kings 18:13)

6. Fill in the blank: James said we are to be _____ of the word; not just hearers only. (James 1:22)

7. Fill in the blank: _____ is the one who moves his neighbor's landmark. (Deuteronomy 27:17)

8. What was Moses' basket floating in when it was found by Pharaoh's daughter? (Exodus 2:5)

9. From what devastated city did Achan steal treasure? (Joshua 6:1; 7:20–21)

10. Fill in the blank: Paul referred to Jesus as the last _____ . (1 Corinthians 15:45)

11. In Nebuchadnezzar's dream image, besides the image's chest, what else was made out of silver? (Daniel 2:32)

12. What does Solomon call himself in Ecclesiastes 1:1? (Ecclesiastes 1:1)

13. What name means "drawn out of the water"? (Exodus 2:10)

14. Who did the people of Lystra insist that Paul was? (Acts 14:12 NIV)

15. Besides Festus, what other governor did Paul appear before? (Acts 24:27)

16. What color robes did those who came out of the great tribulation wear who were around the throne of heaven to serve God day and night in His temple? (Revelation 7:14–15)

17. *Peniel* means having seen what of God's? (Genesis 32:30)

18. Fill in the blank: "The children of Israel went into the midst of the sea upon the _____ ground." (Exodus 14:22)

19. Whom did the wise men ask, "Where is he that is born King of the Jews"? (Matthew 2:1-3)

20. What word means thorns or wood? (Exodus 25:10)

21. God sent manna in response to what specific complaint of the Israelites? (Exodus 16:3)

22. How many queens of Judah are mentioned by name? (2 Kings 11:1)

```
C  X  D  A  R  V  M  P  R  E  A  Q  H  E  R
U  Z  E  Q  P  E  W  R  G  S  E  V  E  N  K
R  S  W  D  R  I  V  E  R  H  F  I  R  U  L
C  E  E  B  A  T  A  G  N  J  K  E  M  R  S
E  V  T  N  S  H  O  N  E  F  A  C  E  E  H
D  E  A  Z  N  S  X  U  P  M  L  N  S  B  I
R  I  V  E  I  A  F  H  O  L  A  O  W  R  T
Y  N  X  W  P  V  C  H  E  T  M  R  E  O  T
D  O  R  E  H  Q  C  H  U  N  I  B  V  A  T
R  A  F  E  L  I  X  Z  E  B  T  J  S  P  I
Y  P  K  B  R  X  T  F  U  R  T  O  R  E  M
Z  P  R  E  A  C  H  E  R  Q  I  W  E  J  D
R  P  J  I  D  S  M  N  Y  T  H  B  O  R  E
F  E  S  Z  A  V  U  C  U  R  S  E  D  K  X
R  M  A  R  M  S  T  H  F  E  L  X  I  J  K
```

Puzzle 11

1. Who was the prophet that literally ate the Word of God? (Ezekiel 2:9–3:3)

2. In Revelation 2:17, the church at Pergamos was told that if they overcame, they would be given what to eat? (Revelation 2:17)

3. Who said "Behold the maidservant of the Lord"? (Luke 1:38)

4. The High Priest could enter the Holy of Holies alone on only what one day of the year? (Leviticus 16:3, 34)

5. Who was Sanballat's cohort when they plotted to trick Nehemiah into leaving his work and meet them? (Nehemiah 6:2–3)

6. How many stones were used to make the memorial to the river crossing? (Joshua 4:4–5)

7. Besides Aquila, who else was a tentmaker? (Acts 18:1–3)

8. How was Joab, the commander for David's army, related to David? (2 Samuel 8:16, 1 Chronicles 2:13–16)

9. Who said that the effective prayers of a righteous man availeth much? (James 5:16)

10. How many days had Lazarus been dead before Jesus arrived at the tomb? (John 11:39)

11. Besides the birds and thorns, what other hazard befell the seeds in Jesus' parable of the sower? (Matthew 13:4–7)

12. Who made a prophecy to the country Edom? (Obadiah 1:1)

13. Paul and Titus were sent to correct problems in which church? (2 Corinthians 8:23)

14. What famous city was near Jerusalem? (John 11:18)

15. The Israelites were to eat with shoes on their feet and where were their staffs supposed to be? (Exodus 12:11)

16. After Jesus prayed to the Father, who did He raise from the dead? (John 11:43)

17. What noisemakers hung off the hem of the priest's garment? (Exodus 28:33–34)

18. Which five virgins had to ask for oil for their lamps? (Matthew 25:8)

19. How many thousands of proverbs did 1 Kings 4:32 say Solomon spoke? (1 Kings 4:32)

20. Who did God say, "Ask! What shall I give you?" (1 Kings 3:5)

21. God told Aaron to stretch out his rod to make the dust of the land into what? (Exodus 8:16)

22. Besides Shemaiah, what other Old Testament prophet also kept genealogies? (2 Chronicles 12:15)

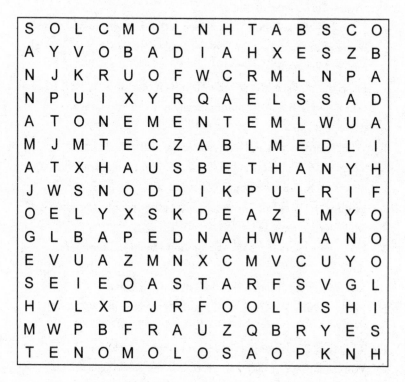

```
S O L C M O L N H T A B S C O
A Y V O B A D I A H X E S Z B
N J K R U O F W C R M L N P A
N P U I X Y R Q A E L S S A D
A T O N E M E N T E M L W U A
M J M T E C Z A B L M E D L I
A T X H A U S B E T H A N Y H
J W S N O D D I K P U L R I F
O E L Y X S K D E A Z L M Y O
G L B A P E D N A H W I A N O
E V U A Z M N X C M V C U Y O
S E I E O A S T A R F S V G L
H V L X D J R F O O L I S H I
M W P B F R A U Z Q B R Y E S
T E N O M O L O S A O P K N H
```

Puzzle 12

1. What king burned the scroll of Jeremiah's prophecies? (Jeremiah 36:9; 25–27)
2. Who were first called "Christians" in Antioch? (Acts 11:26)
3. Besides Simeon, what other son of Jacob helped slay all the males of Shechem's city in retaliation against the city's prince for raping their sister? (Genesis 34:5, 25)
4. Fill in the blank: When Thomas learned Jesus was going to the home of Lazarus, he said, "Let us go also, that we may _____ with him"? (John 11:16)
5. Fill in the blank: in the parable, The Rich Man and _____ , it teaches that being rich doesn't automatically get you into heaven. (Luke 16:19–31)
6. What is prolonged and every vision fails? (Ezekiel 12:22)
7. What historic outpouring of God's Spirit in Jerusalem followed an upper room prayer meeting? (Acts 2:1–4)
8. Besides the prophet Zechariah, what other prophet prophesied while Jerusalem was being rebuilt? (Ezra 5:1)
9. How many years did it take Solomon to build the temple? (1 Kings 6:38)
10. Whose son was Maher-Shalal-Hash-Baz? (Isaiah 8:3)
11. While in Jerusalem, who told Paul of a plot to kill him? (Acts 23:14–16)
12. Who said, "Your people shall be my people"? (Ruth 1:16)
13. Who said that our faith can overcome the world? (1 John 5:4)
14. Who said, "The son of this bondwoman shall not be heir with my son"? (Genesis 21:9–10)
15. What was the name of the pool that Jesus had the blind man wash in after He made clay and put it on the blind man's eyes? (John 9:11)
16. In total, how many times did Joshua's army march around the walls of Jericho? (Joshua 6:3–4)

17. What king made priests from every class of people, an act that destroyed his house? (1 Kings 13:33)

18. The church of Ephesus was told that if they overcame, they would be given to eat from the tree of what? (Revelation 2:7)

19. During the time of the plagues on Egypt, how many days did the plague of darkness cover the land? (Exodus 10:22)

20. To whom did God say, "From where do you come?" (Job 1:7)

21. Fill in the blank: The Jews were made to _____ building "by force and power." (Ezra 4:23)

22. Who was famous for making a detailed organization of temple personnel? (1 Chronicles 23:6)

```
C N D I S C I P L L E H Z A S
E E F I L N X O I Y S H B E E
A E Q W P H Y C F A N Y L A V
C T I T S O C E T N E P A N E
E R U A D J F A Y M I V Z D E
S I L O A M N O I C P Z A X J
P H V E N R Y M S N B V R A E
E T A J E H O I A K I M U I R
N Z X C P U D A R D Q D S L O
T L G C H N T Y A F B A I M B
I F E F E R U T H A I L A E A
C R Z V W A G H V A B U G K O
O D E X I K S R H E W M G V N
S S E S I U J E R O B O A M M
T H I R T E N E H D A Z H X P
```

Puzzle 13

1. The Bible says that what type of man regards the life of an animal? (Proverbs 12:10)

2. Baruch was the servant to which prophet? (Jeremiah 32:12)

3. According to Psalm 119, it says to give me understanding and I shall do what with Your Law? (Psalm 119:34)

4. What was the name of the king of Tyre who sold King Solomon the cedars of Lebanon to use in building the Lord's temple? (1 Kings 5:2–10)

5. When the first heaven and earth pass away, what will no longer exist? (Revelation 21:1)

6. Who did the enemies bribe with eleven hundred pieces of silver each to tell them Samson's secret? (Judges 16:4–5)

7. What Old Testament man had five daughters but no sons and the five daughters won the right to inherit his property when he died? (Numbers 27:1–6)

8. In Revelation 1:20, what did the seven lampstands represent? (Revelation 1:20)

9. Whose slave convinced her master to seek out a prophet of Israel concerning his disease? (2 Kings 5:2–3)

10. Like what on soda is one who sings songs to someone with a heavy heart? (Proverbs 25:20 NKJV)

11. Who was Leah's firstborn? (Genesis 29:32)

12. Who said he obtained mercy because he acted ignorantly in unbelief? (1 Timothy 1:13)

13. The scroll that John was told to eat tasted as sweet as what in his mouth? (Revelation 10:10)

14. Who is called the Chief Shepherd? (1 Peter 5:4)

15. What material was used to make the tent pegs of the tabernacle? (Exodus 27:19)

16. What woman, besides Hannah, was Elkanah's wife? (1 Samuel 1:2)

17. On which side of the Jordan River did the tribes of Reuben, Gad, and the half tribe of Manasseh settle? (Joshua 18:7)

18. From what tribe did Jesus descend? (Matthew 1:3)

19. Fill in the bank: Jesus healed on the Sabbath, indicating that it is _____ to do good on the Sabbath days. (Matthew 12:12)

20. Who defined sin as knowing to do good but not doing it? (James 4:17)

21. How many sons did Esau have? (Genesis 36:4-5)

22. Who was the prostitute/harlot who helped hide the Israelite spies who were spying on the Promised Land? (Joshua 2:1)

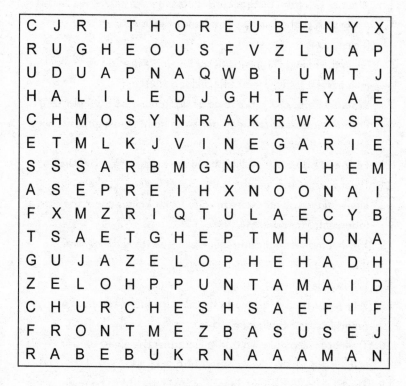

C	J	R	I	T	H	O	R	E	U	B	E	N	Y	X
R	U	G	H	E	O	U	S	F	V	Z	L	U	A	P
U	D	U	A	P	N	A	Q	W	B	I	U	M	T	J
H	A	L	I	L	E	D	J	G	H	T	F	Y	A	E
C	H	M	O	S	Y	N	R	A	K	R	W	X	S	R
E	T	M	L	K	J	V	I	N	E	G	A	R	I	E
S	S	S	A	R	B	M	G	N	O	D	L	H	E	M
A	S	E	P	R	E	I	H	X	N	O	O	N	A	I
F	X	M	Z	R	I	Q	T	U	L	A	E	C	Y	B
T	S	A	E	T	G	H	E	P	T	M	H	O	N	A
G	U	J	A	Z	E	L	O	P	H	E	H	A	D	H
Z	E	L	O	H	P	P	U	N	T	A	M	A	I	D
C	H	U	R	C	H	E	S	H	S	A	E	F	I	F
F	R	O	N	T	M	E	Z	B	A	S	U	S	E	J
R	A	B	E	B	U	K	R	N	A	A	A	M	A	N

Puzzle 14

1. What tribe had a book of the Bible named for them? (Leviticus)
2. Fill in the blank: The Lord gave Solomon _____ as He had promised him? (1 Kings 5:12)
3. What type of vow prevented Samson from ever cutting his hair? (Judges 16:17)
4. How many rivers flowed out of the Garden of Eden? (Genesis 2:10)
5. What book of the Bible recorded Rahab's story? (Joshua 2:1–24)
6. According to the Psalms, God's understanding is what? (Psalm 147:5)
7. Fill in the blank: This city is described in Revelation as "Fallen! Fallen is _____ the Great!" (Revelation 18:2)
8. Who did Peter call "a preacher of righteousness"? (2 Peter 2:5)
9. From what land were the traders who bought Joseph from his brothers? (Genesis 37:28)
10. Fill in the blank: "All we like sheep have gone _____"? (Isaiah 53:6)
11. What was another name for the Sea of Galilee? (Luke 5:1)
12. Linen and goat's hair were used to make what items in the tabernacle? (Exodus 26:1, 7)
13. To what mountain did Abraham take Isaac to sacrifice him? (Genesis 22:2)
14. Where has God put a new song? (Psalm 40:3)
15. Which epistle did Paul write that dealt with the return of a runaway slave? (Philemon 1:10–16)
16. The Lord will gather what with His arms? (Isaiah 40:11)
17. Who was Orpah's sister-in-law? (Ruth 1:14–15)
18. The New Testament says that believers are not to be unequally what with unbelievers? (2 Corinthians 6:14)
19. What tribe settled north and northeast of the Sea of Galilee? (Deuteronomy 33:23)
20. After Job's sons were all killed, how many new sons did God give Job? (Job 42:13)

21. What psalmist spoke of secret sins and presumptuous sins? (Psalm 19:1, 12, 13 NKJV)

22. Fill in the blank: Paul said Jesus is the "chief _____ ." (Ephesians 2:20)

```
P  H  I  L  E  E  M  O  N  B  Y  O  K  E  D
E  O  U  I  N  T  E  N  R  V  A  S  E  K  C
A  T  D  E  O  S  N  I  A  T  R  U  C  M  O
S  F  I  V  E  L  E  R  T  M  T  Q  Z  O  R
G  E  N  N  E  S  A  R  E  T  S  N  X  U  N
M  U  Y  B  I  B  L  E  D  N  A  R  M  T  E
W  O  O  D  S  F  O  U  R  I  V  U  P  H  R
I  V  D  B  E  I  N  U  D  W  E  T  C  T  S
S  B  M  S  T  A  Y  I  L  A  T  H  P  A  N
D  A  Z  T  I  P  M  N  S  E  V  E  N  U  O
L  B  X  A  R  W  A  T  E  R  J  I  G  H  N
O  Y  Z  H  A  O  N  X  W  E  R  O  D  S  E
M  L  A  T  Z  O  O  P  H  I  L  E  M  O  N
M  O  R  I  A  H  I  W  T  X  P  C  A  J  E
E  N  W  E  N  O  T  S  R  E  N  R  O  C  Y
```

PUZZLE 15

1. Fill in the blank: Daniel _____ in his heart that he would not defile himself. (Daniel 1:8)

2. After Jesus sent the multitude away and the disciples crossed by ship to the other side without Jesus, what did they see Him doing on the sea during the fourth watch of the night? (Mark 6:48–49)

3. After Esther became queen, who found favor by foiling an assassination attempt on the king? (Esther 2:21–23)

4. Besides singing, what else did the Israelites immediately do after the Lord brought them out of Egypt? (Exodus 15:20)

5. Who used a fable about the king of trees to prove that he was supposed to be in charge? (Judges 9:1, 7–15)

6. How many days old was Jesus when He was taken to the temple to be presented? (Luke 2:21)

7. Fill in the blank: Jesus said He came not to _____ the Law but to fulfill it? (Matthew 5:17)

8. Who was known as "the son of perdition"? (John 17:12)

9. Which prophet prophesied the Messiah would be led as a lamb to the slaughter? (Isaiah 53:7)

10. In Nebuchadnezzar's dream image, besides the image's belly, what else was made out of the material bronze? (Daniel 2:32 NIV)

11. What occupation did blind Bartimaeus have when Jesus gave him sight? (Mark 10:46)

12. What name means "the mighty hunter"? (Genesis 10:9)

13. When God caused the army of Syria to flee, what disease did the four people who looted the deserted Syrian camp have? (2 Kings 7:3, 8)

14. What was Abednego's Hebrew name? (Daniel 1:7)

15. According to Revelation 7:14–15, where is God day and night so that those who came out of the great tribulation can serve Him? (Revelation 7:14–15)

16. What book in the Old Testament foretold that Jesus would be born in Bethlehem? (Micah 5:2)

17. What was Nehemiah's occupation to the king? (Nehemiah 1:11)
18. Besides iron, what other material did Tubal-cain work with? (Genesis 4:22)
19. What relation to Potiphar falsely accused Joseph of an improper sexual advance? (Genesis 39:7)
20. Where will God ultimately bring Lucifer down to? (Isaiah 14:15 NKJV)
21. What did Jesus do at Lazarus' death? (John 11:35)
22. What was the name of Abraham's sister who was stricken with leprosy because she spoke against his second wife? (Numbers 12:10)

```
C M O R D S I C A I X E A J O
U M I C A H X U S T O R E S W
P R Q E I G H T W A L K I N G
B D L A B I M E L E C H N U L
A E A Z S H E O L P E S V N E
E C V A S T P B R T A P M A P
R N I R E U R O D B W I F E
E A I I X Q R E U R E B R Z S
H D S A T R P J A T N C I V T
H D F H P A O S Z Q W B A E R
T R P L K G S N M D O R M I N
R U N I N G E Y A A S P O T P
Y O R T S E D R D B L F N H A
X K C U P B E A R E R C V N L
P U P O S E D Y S O R P E L M
```

Puzzle 16

1. What does "Nazarite" mean? (Numbers 6:2)

2. The people Jesus drove out of the temple were changing what? (Mark 11:15)

3. What prophet was called "the Tishbite"? (1 Kings 17:1)

4. Who planned to take two mule loads of earth (dirt) back to Syria after he was healed of his leprosy? (2 Kings 5:17)

5. According to Micah 6:8, how are we to walk with God? (Micah 6:8)

6. Fill in the blank: Blessed are they that mourn: for they shall be _____ . (Matthew 5:4)

7. Who was the wife of the governor Felix? (Acts 24:24)

8. John described the Lamb he saw in heaven as having seven eyes and seven of what other feature? (Revelation 5:6)

9. Besides Paul's epistle to the Colossians, what other epistle did Paul write that told children to obey their parents? (Ephesians 6:1)

10. The moneychangers had made the temple a den of thieves but it should have been called what kind of house by all nations? (Mark 11:17)

11. In Nebuchadnezzar's dream image, what part of the image was made of iron? (Daniel 2:33)

12. While in the wilderness, the Lord went before the Israelites by day in a pillar of cloud and by night, what was the pillar made of? (Exodus 13:21)

13. During the reign of Esther, what was another word for "the lot"? (Esther 9:24)

14. Who was called "the father of all who played the harp and flute"? (Genesis 4:21)

15. After Esther agreed to meet the king, she told Mordecai to tell her people to do what for three days? (Esther 4:16)

16. Malachi says the Sun of Righteousness shall rise with what in His wings? (Malachi 4:2)

17. *Mizpah* means who watches between you and me? (Genesis 31:49)

18. How did the disciples react when Jesus calmed the angry winds and water on the Sea of Galilee? (Matthew 8:27)

19. Fill in the blank: In order to build the tabernacle, the Israelites brought a _____ offering. (Exodus 35:29 NKJV)

20. Who had the second longest recorded lifespan, 962 years? (Genesis 5:20)

21. What did Amos do before he became a prophet? (Amos 1:1)

22. Name the Lamb's record (of Life) of all who are saved? (Revelation 21:27)

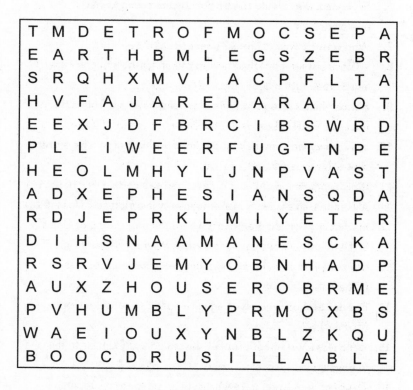

```
T  M  D  E  T  R  O  F  M  O  C  S  E  P  A
E  A  R  T  H  B  M  L  E  G  S  Z  E  B  R
S  R  Q  H  X  M  V  I  A  C  P  F  L  T  A
H  V  F  A  J  A  R  E  D  A  R  A  I  O  T
E  E  X  J  D  F  B  R  C  I  B  S  W  R  D
P  L  L  I  W  E  E  R  F  U  G  T  N  P  E
H  E  O  L  M  H  Y  L  J  N  P  V  A  S  T
A  D  X  E  P  H  E  S  I  A  N  S  Q  D  A
R  D  J  E  P  R  K  L  M  I  Y  E  T  F  R
D  I  H  S  N  A  A  M  A  N  E  S  C  K  A
R  S  R  V  J  E  M  Y  O  B  N  H  A  D  P
A  U  X  Z  H  O  U  S  E  R  O  B  R  M  E
P  V  H  U  M  B  L  Y  P  R  M  O  X  B  S
W  A  E  I  O  U  X  Y  N  B  L  Z  K  Q  U
B  O  O  C  D  R  U  S  I  L  L  A  B  L  E
```

Puzzle 17

1. When did Nicodemus, a Pharisee, come to see Jesus? (John 3:1-2)

2. Whose wife told him to curse God and die? (Job 2:9)

3. Who defeated the prophets of Baal on Mount Carmel when fire fell from heaven? (1 Kings 18:17-19)

4. In Daniel's vision, how many weeks were determined? (Daniel 9:24)

5. Who did God ask, "Is it right for you to be angry?" (Jonah 4:9)

6. In Revelation 2:11, the church at Syrma was told that if they overcame, they would not be hurt by the second what? (Revelation 2:11)

7. Who was Abraham's father? (Genesis 11:31)

8. What priest kept Joash safe when all of Joash's siblings were killed? (2 Kings 11:1-4)

9. About which plague did Pharaoh's magicians say, "This is the finger of God"? (Exodus 8:18-19)

10. In all, how many times did the men of Joshua's army give a great shout? (Joshua 6:10, 16)

11. Which companion of Paul's is described as a certain Jew born in Alexandria, an eloquent man, and mighty in scriptures? (Acts 18:24)

12. In what city was the Pentecost where the outpouring of God's Spirit followed an upper room prayer meeting? (Acts 2:1-5)

13. Who did Paul say tried to keep him from making progress? (1 Thessalonians 2:18)

14. Besides Jeshua, who else began to build the house of God again? (Ezra 5:2)

15. Which Old Testament prophet described a city similar to the one in Revelation 21? (Ezekiel 48:30-35)

16. The people of Israel gave what type of offering to supply the materials to build the tabernacle? (Exodus 35:29 NKJV)

17. Which New Testament writer said we are a holy and royal priesthood? (1 Peter 2:5, 9)

18. In Jesus' parable, who found a pearl and sold all he had to buy it? (Matthew 13:45–46)

19. Whom did Jesus say, "Whosoever liveth and believeth in me shall never die. Believest thou this?" (John 11:24–26)

20. Who said, "Thou art the man"? (2 Samuel 12:7)

21. How many soils are described in the parable of the sower? (Matthew 13:4–8)

22. Who refused to come when her husband, the king, called for her join him at his royal feast to show off her beauty? (Esther 1:12)

A	S	N	I	G	H	H	T	B	E	Z	E	I	K	E
P	E	T	E	R	C	F	N	A	T	A	S	E	D	L
D	V	B	C	H	O	N	C	E	P	N	C	F	K	D
V	E	T	D	U	N	V	R	S	K	I	I	J	N	M
A	N	F	R	E	E	W	I	L	L	O	N	G	H	A
S	T	M	D	L	A	M	B	I	X	R	Y	T	H	R
C	Y	E	Q	E	Z	T	M	E	R	C	H	A	N	T
A	T	L	P	Z	U	M	H	O	R	S	E	D	Y	H
D	W	A	T	E	R	A	H	U	U	L	G	I	T	A
A	G	S	N	K	J	B	A	P	O	L	L	O	S	P
I	S	U	A	I	Q	O	W	E	R	T	Y	H	O	I
O	F	R	L	E	B	A	B	B	U	R	E	Z	E	G
H	N	E	M	L	A	U	G	H	I	N	G	J	K	H
E	B	J	O	N	A	H	V	C	X	Z	S	D	T	Y
J	W	I	T	H	S	A	V	P	N	A	T	H	A	N

Puzzle 18

1. To whom did Paul command, "Be careful for nothing; but in everything by prayer and supplication with thanksgiving let your requests be known unto God"? (Philippians 4:6)

2. After Esther agreed to speak to the king, she told Mordecai to tell her people to do what for three days? (Esther 4:16)

3. Philip had how many daughters who prophesied? (Acts 21:8-9)

4. What prophet told an adulterous king the parable of a man with one ewe lamb? (2 Samuel 12:1-14)

5. Where were the words "Holiness to the Lord" engraved on the High Priest's turban? (Exodus 28:36-38)

6. When they were entering the Promised Land, the priests blew trumpets that were made out of horns of what animal? (Joshua 6:4)

7. Who was Paul's companion who chronicled much of Paul's missionary activities in Acts? (Acts 1:1; 16:10; Colossians 4:14)

8. Jesus told us to be of good what because He has overcome the world? (John 16:33)

9. To whom did God say, "How have I wearied you?" (Micah 6:3)

10. In a proverb, who returns to his own vomit? (2 Peter 2:22)

11. Besides linen, what type of animal hair was also used to make the curtains in the tabernacle? (Exodus 26:7)

12. Besides fasting and laying their hands on Paul and Barnabas, what else did the church at Antioch do to set them apart for missionary service? (Acts 13:3)

13. To which Mary was Jesus speaking when He said, "Woman, why weepest thou?" (John 20:1, 15)

14. What separated the Holy Place from the Most Holy Place? (Exodus 26:33)

15. To whom did God say, "Whom shall I send, and who will go for Us?" (Isaiah 6:8)

16. After Jericho's success, the Israelites failed at first to take what small city? (Joshua 7:4-5)

17. In Revelation 2:26, the church at Thyatira was told that if they overcame, they would be given power over what? (Revelation 2:26)

18. The ark of the covenant was carried by what type people from the tribe of Levi? (Joshua 3:3)

19. Who said this, "Vanity of vanity; all is vanity"? (Ecclesiastes 1:1–2)

20. Fill in the blank: the Roman commander called for soldiers, horsemen, and spearmen to safely take Paul to Governor Felix in the city of _____ ? (Acts 23:23–24)

21. Whose daughters were said to be the most beautiful in the land? (Job 42:15)

22. Which part of Egypt was set apart so that the swarms of flies didn't go there? (Exodus 8:22)

```
I  P  F  C  H  E  E  R  K  A  J  I  S  R
S  V  L  U  A  R  S  T  S  E  I  R  P  F  A
A  B  U  G  C  A  S  O  P  I  U  Y  T  F  E
B  S  K  H  M  A  G  D  A  L  E  N  E  D  L
A  Z  E  X  F  T  E  A  V  B  P  M  L  C  D
P  E  N  J  A  B  M  S  H  P  R  E  I  F  L
R  X  W  O  M  U  Q  N  A  G  A  F  T  D  E
A  Z  G  B  M  N  T  A  X  R  V  L  P  S  K
Y  R  P  K  B  O  V  T  S  M  E  H  N  J  Y
E  W  Q  P  H  I  L  I  P  P  I  A  N  S  M
D  Z  X  H  G  B  K  O  O  L  I  M  I  K
G  O  S  H  E  N  K  N  S  V  B  A  P  D  R
Z  C  G  U  V  P  B  S  I  E  R  S  F  K  U
Y  R  N  A  H  T  A  N  X  B  M  I  N  L  O
C  A  E  S  A  E  R  R  E  R  T  N  O  R  F
```

Puzzle 19

1. The figures inside the oracle where the ark of the covenant was placed were in the shape of what? (1 Kings 6:23)

2. Circumcision was a sign of the covenant between God and who else? (Genesis 17:9)

3. According to the Bible, what does a man of understanding have? (Proverbs 10:23)

4. Which tribe, according to Jacob's blessing, was "a hind/deer let loose"? (Genesis 49:21)

5. Jesus said that where your treasure is, there your what will be? (Matthew 6:21)

6. Who set the ark of the covenant on the great and large stone? (1 Samuel 6:15)

7. What grandson of Noah had a name that became symbolic for all those who would try to destroy God's people? (Genesis 10:2)

8. Who was buried in the cave that Abraham bought for a burial place many years before? (Genesis 49:33; 50:13)

9. Who saw the vision of a sheet filled with unclean animals? (Acts 10:9–17)

10. After Moses died and Joshua was now the leader, the two spies were sent out from where? (Joshua 2:1)

11. Fill in the blank: Jesus said, "The good _____ giveth his life for the sheep." (John 10:11)

12. The Israelites were to set free any Hebrew slave once every how many years? (Deuteronomy 15:12)

13. Which of Solomon's children became king? (1 Kings 11:43)

14. When God asked Satan where he had come from, what did he respond? (Job 1:7)

15. What disciple of Jesus had the same name as one of the tribes? (Matthew 9:9, Mark 2:14)

16. Who said, "To obey is better than sacrifice?" (1 Samuel 15:22)

17. The spies said the Promised Land flowed with milk and what else? (Numbers 13:27)
18. Who sang a song with Barak after the Canaanite king was defeated? (Judges 5:1)
19. We make God what if we say we have not sinned? (1 John 1:10)
20. Which son of Jacob convinced his brothers to sell Joseph into slavery? (Genesis 37:26-27)
21. Who was commanded to eat the scroll which ended up tasting as sweet as honey in his mouth? (Revelation 10:9-10)
22. In what country was the River Chebar located in? (Ezekiel 1:1)

S	L	E	I	G	N	O	O	D	L	E	L	U	C	E
Z	E	X	M	A	G	O	G	I	D	O	U	G	H	P
F	V	K	A	U	D	R	L	I	S	T	R	A	E	H
T	I	R	H	T	R	A	E	Y	R	A	K	E	R	F
P	T	S	E	I	T	A	Z	E	B	R	A	J	U	R
Y	E	N	O	H	B	C	H	I	N	A	U	V	B	I
W	S	X	P	Q	O	M	N	H	Y	W	B	C	I	A
W	E	A	I	D	E	B	O	R	A	H	L	K	M	M
E	N	H	N	K	R	J	O	B	E	P	X	I	O	U
H	E	F	T	A	J	H	O	A	G	E	T	Z	D	S
T	V	Q	I	T	H	C	A	T	M	T	N	M	S	O
T	E	L	N	Z	A	J	M	H	I	E	P	T	I	U
T	S	C	Y	J	D	M	A	H	A	R	B	A	W	N
A	V	B	N	M	U	P	S	H	E	P	H	E	R	D
M	V	A	S	E	J	L	E	U	M	A	S	A	N	D

Puzzle 20

1. The tribes Judah and Benjamin were gathering together and planning to make war against Israel to regain the kingdom for which king? (1 Kings 12:21)

2. Jesus described the one who enters the sheepfold other than by the door as a robber and what else? (John 10:1)

3. Who sang her song of praise to the Lord when she dedicated Samuel to the Lord? (1 Samuel 1:28–2:1)

4. Who was the ancestor to the giants in the land of Canaan? (Numbers 13:33)

5. Paul had what cut off because he had taken a vow? (Acts 18:18)

6. Besides Solomon, what other king also wrote psalms? (Psalm 62)

7. The tribes of Ephraim and Manasseh received the land allotment for which tribe? (Joshua 16:1, 4)

8. How many times did Satan tempt Jesus? (Matthew 4:1–11)

9. Which prophet decried against how the Israelites were offering blind animals as sacrifices? (Malachi 1:8)

10. Rahab was to mark her house with what color thread? (Joshua 2:18, 21)

11. Besides Moses, who else appeared and talked to Jesus at the Transfiguration? (Matthew 17:3)

12. Fill in the blank: One of the proverbs says we should not lean on our _____ understanding. (Proverbs 3:5)

13. The Sermon on the Mount is contained in three chapters in what book of the Bible? (Matthew 5–7)

14. Fill in the blank: The Lord said, " _____ like a river"? (Isaiah 66:12)

15. What was the name of the slave that Paul referred to when he wrote his epistle that dealt with the return of a runaway slave? (Philemon 10)

16. How many shekels of silver did Joseph's brothers sell him for? (Genesis 37:28)

17. The sign Gideon asked of God involved a what? (Judges 6:37)

18. What was the name of Jacob's one daughter? (Genesis 34:1)

19. Who brought the ark of the covenant into the temple after it was completed? (1 Kings 8:6)

20. What famous naughty girl in the Old Testament lived in the Valley of Sorek? (Judges 16:4)

21. Who was Methuselah's grandson? (Genesis 5:25, 29)

22. When he went to fight Goliath, how many stones did David take out of the brook? (1 Samuel 17:40)

```
C A S T Z D I V A D X V W H M
D P T A J S N B X I E F V A E
A F S D O E A W Q C N M L O X
S D E C S N B H A N N A H N I
H A I R E B E E P Y C X N N D
A V R C P Q P S X H Z M W A N
N J P G H F P R I C E O B L K
I D R E H O B O A M A Z S C P
D R F P A O I B S A U C C E E
W Q V P L E A S E T D S A X A
W H A J I L E U K T Y O R U S
N U I T L E X T H H A N L K E
T H R E E V B I W E C E E L F
D S J N D I E L T W E N T Y K
F R T W Z F O N E S E M U S V
```

Puzzle 21

1. What offering was continual? (Exodus 29:38, 42)

2. Besides Emim, what other word refers to giants? (Deuteronomy 2:11)

3. Who was captain of Pharaoh's guard during Joseph's youth? (Genesis 39:1)

4. What material was the king's scepter that he had to extend to Queen Esther when she came unannounced so she wouldn't be killed? (Esther 4:11)

5. Fill in the blank: Jesus came to _____ those under the Law. (Galatians 4:4-5)

6. Jesus described Himself as the Bread of what after feeding the five thousand men? (John 6:10, 35)

7. Which disciple actually entered the empty tomb? (John 20:6)

8. What part of the late Joseph did Moses and the Israelites take with them when they left Egypt? (Exodus 13:19)

9. Besides iron, what else were the feet in Nebuchadnezzar's dream image made of? (Daniel 2:33)

10. Who did the people of Lystra insist was Zeus? (Acts 14:12)

11. What town were Mary and Joseph living in when the angel announced to her that she would be having the child to be named Jesus? (Luke 1:26-27)

12. Who was the cupbearer to King Artaxerxes? (Nehemiah 1:11)

13. What word defines "Sabbath"? (Genesis 2:2 AMP)

14. Who was famous for saying "As for me and my house, we will serve the Lord"? (Joshua 24:2, 15)

15. Psalm 69:21 mentions what that was offered to Jesus on the cross? (Psalm 69:21)

16. What word means "house of God"? (Genesis 28:17-19)

17. After the rich ruler said he had obeyed all of the commands from his youth to the present, who did Jesus say the rich ruler should sell all of his goods and give it to? (Luke 18:22)

18. John likened his first glimpse of the holy city, new Jerusalem, as what adorned for her husband? (Revelation 21:2)

19. What was Belteshazzar's Hebrew name? (Daniel 1:7)

20. What was the occupation of Reuel (Jethro) of Midian? (Exodus 2:16–18)

21. Who did John the Baptist call "the Lamb of God"? (John 1:29)

22. What one did Paul tell the Thessalonians was coming with "all power and signs and lying wonders"? (2 Thessalonians 2:9 NIV)

```
S D C Z A Y A R N H W P B V A
R A E I R A H P I T O P R A Y
X P G A L L X T M Y U B W R L
P R O U X C D A N I E L B N E
A I L H J Z O T I B K M U K S
S A D T R O O P J B F A R X S
T Q J E S U S C E A S I N G L
W E L R S Y R H V R B N T A A
R P T A H Q E C U N E A B M W
E Z D Z W H D A X A I T J L N
S C W A U L E V K B O N E S E
A D R N E H E M I A H H R P S
B O I F J Y M S W S T X F B M
P R I E S T X Q S E D O N K Y
O L H G E D I R B L A U M B W
```

Puzzle 22

1. When Naaman was healed of his leprosy, how many mule loads of earth was he planning to take back with him to Syria? (2 Kings 5:17)

2. Back in Jesus' day, what coin was worth a day's wage? (Matthew 20:2)

3. What name in the Old Testament meant "churl"? (1 Samuel 25:3, 25)

4. When a voice from heaven said "Blessed are the dead which die in the Lord from henceforth," it meant that they would be resting from what? (Revelation 14:13)

5. When Moses blessed the tribes before his death, which tribe did he say dwelt like a lion? (Deuteronomy 33:22)

6. Potiphar's wife made an improper sexual advance upon who? (Genesis 39:7–12)

7. When Jesus stated "I must work the works of him that sent me, while it is day: the night cometh, when no man can work," He was describing Himself as the Light of what? (John 9:4–5)

8. What name in Hebrew means "angel of the bottomless pit"? (Revelation 9:11)

9. What was Meshach's Hebrew name? (Daniel 1:7)

10. Fill in the blank: Jesus said that not a _____ or a tittle will pass away from the Law until it is fulfilled. (Matthew 5:18)

11. Nebuchadnezzar's astrologers were unable to give an interpretation because he would not tell them the contents of what? (Daniel 2:1–9)

12. Who was Noah's father? (Genesis 5:28–29)

13. A sleepy young man named Eutychus fell from what during a sermon by Paul? (Acts 20:9–12)

14. What occupation did Festus have? (Acts 24:27)

15. What surname meant "sons of thunder"? (Mark 3:17)

16. Esau was born looking like what color? (Genesis 25:25)

17. What relation of Pharaoh pulled baby Moses out of the river? (Exodus 2:5)

18. What type of vow meant they were not allowed to drink wine or vinegar? (Numbers 6:2–3)

19. Fill in the blank: Revelation 3:14 says Jesus is the _____ , faithful and true. (Revelation 3:14)

20. The silversmiths in Ephesus made shrines to what goddess? (Acts 19:24)

21. Fill in the blank: Esther said, "I will go to the king, even though it is against the law. And if I _____ , I perish." (Esther 4:16)

22. Besides John, who else was a "son of thunder"? (Mark 3:17)

```
W O D N I W Z X D E R I G T H
T C F S Y W O R L D N M O I X
K W D W Q C R A B I T J V P K
V M O S B J B P J X A Z E E K
C I V R W O R K S B A P R M L
K S D X R S A L A B A N N A A
M H N S B E V N A C X D O N N
F A D U S P W D E A E Z R A D
P E R I S H D I G R G H D I M
P L K R J O R E T H G U A D A
M I U A N Y R E W N Q E R Z R
E V C N A Z A R I T E E S X K
A H C E M A L B N M A S L K J
R Q A D S D F S E M A J S G H
D W E T O I L S R F I S H T P
```

PUZZLE 23

1. When Paul was near death in prison, whom did he urge to "come before winter"? (2 Timothy 4:21)

2. Who said, "As for me and my house, we will serve the Lord"? (Joshua 24:15)

3. Where did Jesus spend the night praying before choosing the apostles? (Luke 6:12-13)

4. Who was banished to till the ground as punishment for disobeying God in the Garden of Eden? (Genesis 3:23-24)

5. In Revelation 3:5, the church of Sardis was told that if they did overcome, they would be clothed in what items that are white? (Revelation 3:5 NKJV)

6. What prophet's bones revived a dead man? (2 Kings 13:21)

7. Besides Haggai, what other prophet was prophesying in Jerusalem as it was being rebuilt? (Ezra 5:1)

8. Pharaoh's magicians couldn't stand before Moses because they were covered in what? (Exodus 9:11)

9. Besides Abihu, what other son of Aaron was devoured by fire? (Leviticus 10:1-2)

10. Who killed all of Ahab's household, including the priests? (2 Kings 10:11)

11. Fill in the blank: After being struck while before the Sanhedrin, Paul said, "God will strike you, you _____ wall." (Acts 23:3)

12. Which king really hated the prophets Elijah and Micaiah? (1 Kings 21:20; 22:8)

13. In Jesus's illustration of how God wants to give us good things, what did the Lord say a father would not give his son if he asked for bread? (Luke 11:11)

14. Who did God ask, "Is anything too hard for the Lord?" (Genesis 18:14)

15. Who told the Israelites to prepare their hearts for the Lord? (1 Samuel 7:3)

16. What material was to be used to make the tent pegs of the tabernacle? (Exodus 27:19)

17. Who did Jesus ask, "Do you love Me more than these?" (John 21:15)

18. In the parable of The Good Samaritan, the man who was robbed and beaten came from what city with the intention of traveling to Jericho? (Luke 10:30)

19. Under the ground inside what was Achan's plunder secretly hidden? (Joshua 7:21)

20. How many years had Paul been in Rome when the book of Acts ended? (Acts 28:30)

21. What prophet had two children whose names meant "not loved" and "not my people"? (Hosea 1:6, 9)

22. Where were the twelve loaves of the Bread of Presence, or shewbread, supposed to be in the tabernacle Sabbath after Sabbath? (Leviticus 24:5-6)

```
Z B X B C R O W T N M L K E J
G R E A T T F Z G B O I L S H
N A D S N A Q E W N E B R T Y
I S J E H U Z C X P A O I U E
L S T E C A H O T X D V B N
P J K L R M S A M U E L A N O
M A D A M U L R K H J H G B T
U E T R E W S I S Q A S R D S
J S M O U N T A I N Y E U T I
D O F G H J W H L K T P N I O
A H S I L E S A Z E X E C M V
H Z X H T C V B P N M M N O B
A F G I U H J K L R T E E T H
B D H S Q A B R A H A M W H E
P W I N D O W G O I U Y T Y R
```

PUZZLE 24

1. What was the name of the High Priest during Nehemiah's time who built the Sheep Gate? (Nehemiah 3:1)

2. Fill in the blank: After seeing the son of the widow of Nain raised from the dead, the people said, "A great _____ is risen up among us." (Luke 7:16)

3. Which traveling companion was sent by Paul to correct problems in the church at Corinth? (2 Corinthians 8:22–23)

4. Who was King David's great-great-grandmother? (Matthew 1:5)

5. Who did Jesus ask, "What is that to you?" (John 21:21–22)

6. The lamb of the first Passover was to be male or female? (Exodus 12:5)

7. What king, of the lineage of Medes, was made king over the Chaldeans, also known as the Babylonians? (Daniel 9:1)

8. What son of Shealtiel is credited with helping to rebuild the temple after the Babylonian captivity? (Ezra 3:2)

9. What animal killed a prophet who ate and drank when God told him not to? (1 Kings 13:20–24)

10. Whose wife was the daughter of an Egyptian priest? (Genesis 41:45)

11. Whose sons were accused of taking bribes and perverting justice? (1 Samuel 8:1–3)

12. Which wind brought the locusts as one of the plagues on Egypt? (Exodus 10:13)

13. While carrying the ark, who stood in the middle of the Jordan River while all of Israel crossed over? (Joshua 3:17)

14. Who asked "What is truth?" (John 18:38)

15. In Revelation 3:12 the church at Philadelphia was told that if they overcame, they would become what in the temple of God? (Revelation 3:12)

16. What woman did Peter raise from the dead through the name of Jesus Christ? (Acts 9:36–41)

17. Samuel was born as an answer to what? (1 Samuel 1:19, 27)
18. What king did the prophet Nathan help anoint? (1 Kings 1:34)
19. Besides the sun and the thorns, what other hazard was in Jesus' parable of The Sower? (Matthew 13:4-7)
20. Who responded "My punishment is greater than I can bear" when the Lord told him he was "cursed from the earth" for killing his brother? (Genesis 4:11, 13)
21. How many Old Testament prophets raised a boy from the dead? (1 Kings 17:17-24; 2 Kings 4:32-37)
22. What king destroyed the Lord's temple that Solomon built? (2 Kings 24:11)

```
R  A  H  O  B  L  E  B  A  B  B  U  R  E  Z
B  P  O  W  E  R  V  R  R  E  T  E  P  C  A
N  P  M  T  L  P  R  A  Y  E  R  K  I  J  B
T  R  A  P  A  S  H  Z  D  M  F  G  L  H  E
Q  I  W  B  R  A  N  Z  T  S  A  E  A  E  L
L  E  B  A  B  I  R  E  Z  U  Y  L  T  T  R
I  S  O  I  P  Z  H  N  X  J  O  S  E  P  H
S  T  M  N  R  P  B  D  V  B  I  B  L  E  C
A  S  L  K  O  D  J  A  A  H  G  F  D  S  S
M  T  O  R  R  E  S  H  A  R  E  W  Q  R  A
U  Y  P  L  D  O  R  C  A  S  I  N  U  A  I
E  C  V  E  O  B  N  U  N  M  O  U  P  L  O
L  X  I  Z  A  M  S  B  D  I  F  G  S  L  H
S  U  T  I  T  J  O  E  L  I  A  S  H  I  B
Q  K  L  P  O  C  A  N  D  Y  I  C  Y  P  W
```

Puzzle 25

1. Paul said we can become slaves to what for holiness? (Romans 6:19)
2. Whose body did Michael fight with Satan over? (Jude 9)
3. How many sons did David have? (1 Chronicles 3:4, 5, 8)
4. What was the name of King Saul's cousin who was the commander of his army? (1 Samuel 14:50)
5. What was the name of the bronze serpent that Moses made while in the wilderness? (2 Kings 18:4)
6. In order to kill three thousand Philistines, Samson destroyed what structures of a crowded house, causing it to collapse? (Judges 16:29-30)
7. Who vowed to sacrifice to God whatever came out of his house first to greet him? (Judges 11:30-31)
8. How many years did it take Solomon to build the Lord's temple? (1 Kings 6:38)
9. What New Testament person cut off his hair because he had taken a vow? (Acts 18:18)
10. The parable of the lost sheep can be found in Luke and what other book of the Bible? (Matthew 18:12)
11. What we refer to today as the Dead Sea was called what in the Bible? (Deuteronomy 3:17)
12. What patriarch used a stone for a pillow? (Genesis 28:11)
13. To whom was Jesus speaking when He said, "I will strike the Shepherd, and the sheep of the flock will be scattered"? (Matthew 26:31)
14. When the sons of Jacob went to Egypt for the first time, which one was left as a hostage? (Genesis 42:24)
15. In the city described in Revelation 21, twelve of what kind of item represent the twelve tribes of Israel? (Revelation 21:12)
16. What garden did the River Euphrates flow out of? (Genesis 2:10, 14)

17. While in exile, Ezekiel made a model of and laid siege works against what city? (Ezekiel 4:1–2)

18. Whom did God say was blameless and upright and didn't sin with his lips? (Job 1:8; 2:10)

19. Jeremiah prophesied that the Valley of Hinnom would be called the Valley of what? (Jeremiah 7:32)

20. Paul joined how many men who had taken a vow? (Acts 21:23–26)

21. Who was the famous brother to James, Joses, Juda, and Simon? (Mark 6:3)

22. Who saw four living creatures in his vision? (Ezekiel 1:5)

```
S E A L X N O E M I S J E P H
E K Z E V R J D X C V F S B N
S M R I G H T E O U S N E S S
O L J K H G F N P D D Q T A W
M T R E D R A W E H T T A M E
D N Y Z U I F R O M T O G P R
P I P E S C X Z S E K H L N E
E N S E V E N R V L B S A L T
L E K C S N A E L A M T N H H
S T A Y I L J N G S S J O B G
I E H E L P D B O U S E O F U
C E D I S M L A H R Q C F W A
S N P A U L Y E T E A R O E L
I U P V B X N Z S J E S U S S
D D N A T H S U H E N Z R W L
```

PUZZLE 26

1. What was the first tribe to set foot in the Promised Land? (Joshua 3:6)

2. According to the Proverbs, a man's heart plans his ways but the Lord directs what? (Proverbs 16:9)

3. What Old Testament person described a worthless shepherd as one who leaves the flock? (Zechariah 11:17)

4. In Ezekiel's vision in the valley, what objects came together with a rattling sound? (Ezekiel 37:4-7)

5. For those who overcome, their new names are promised to be written on what color stone? (Revelation 2:17)

6. Who prayed to die along with the Philistines? (Judges 16:30)

7. Fill in the blank: The psalmist said God gives His people drink from the river of His _____ . (Psalm 36:8 NIV)

8. Besides Elisha, who else saw the army of the Lord? (Revelation 19:14)

9. Fill in the blank: What man of you, having an hundred sheep, if he lose one of them, doth not leave the ninety and nine in the wilderness, and go after that which is lost, until he _____ it? (Luke 15:4)

10. The psalmist offered God the sacrifice of what? (Psalm 116:17)

11. Who was King Manasseh's father? (2 Kings 20:21)

12. When Joseph made himself known to his brothers, which brother did he embrace first? (Genesis 45:14)

13. What were all the unclean animals on in Peter's vision? (Acts 10:9-17)

14. What Old Testament man unknowingly slept with his own daughter-in-law and later accused her of being a harlot? (Genesis 38:14-26)

15. Besides Bezaleel, what other workman did God appoint to make the things needed to build the tabernacle and clothe the priests? (Exodus 31:6)

16. Fill in the blank: Throughout the book of Ezekiel, the prophet is addressed by the Lord as "the ___ of man." (Ezekiel 2:3)

17. Who was the son of Nun? (Exodus 33:11)

18. The Bible says that in the Garden of Eden, what animal was more subtle and cunning than any beast of the field? (Genesis 3:1)

19. Fill in the blank: The Sermon on the Mount starts with what we call the ___. (Matthew 5:1–12)

20. What was the name of the valley that David and Goliath fought in? (1 Samuel 17:2)

21. Who destroyed the Lord's temple that Solomon built? (2 Kings 24:11–14)

22. Who said, "My sin is always before me?" (Psalm 51:1, 3)

```
Z C L O U D Y X L S C D S N A
S N E A K K L M N E B A V G K
J E H S A M S O N D V V N G E
C S R M O U N T A U N I S D F
R V I P H E R A Q T V D W E S
O U Y Z E C H A R I A H T R T
P S O N Z N I O G T P E L A H
W H I T E B T S V A C X N Z G
N E M L K J K H P E A K I G I
S E W F I N D G A B S D M F L
E T E N A H O L I A B R A T E
N P O H H I U A U H S O J Y D
O U T O D A Y Z X C V B N N M
B G H J U D A H K L S T E P S
D R A Z Z E N D A H C U B E N
```

Puzzle 27

1. Who was the king of Bashan? (Deuteronomy 4:47)
2. What does "Cephas" mean? (John 1:42)
3. What occupation did Demetrius have when he was employed to make shrines? (Acts 19:24)
4. What was the reason why Mary and Joseph had to go to Bethlehem to be registered? (Luke 2:2, 15 NIV)
5. Who was appointed governor of Judah by King Nebuchadnezzar? (Jeremiah 40:5)
6. Psalm 69:9 is a prophecy about Jesus cleansing what? (Psalm 69:9; John 2:13-22)
7. What did Moses stretch out over the sea to divide the waters? (Exodus 14:21)
8. Whose spirit was brought up from the dead by the witch of Endor? (1 Samuel 28:11-14)
9. How did God reveal the secret to Nebuchadnezzar's dream to Daniel at night? (Daniel 2:19)
10. What does Jesus say we are when He is the vine? (John 15:1, 5)
11. Who said if our earthly house is destroyed, "we have a building from God, a house not made with hands, eternal in the heavens"? (2 Corinthians 5:1 NKJV)
12. What was the last of the four words mysteriously written on the wall? (Daniel 5:25)
13. Besides Felix, who else was a governor in the book of Acts? (Acts 24:27)
14. What does Anathema mean? (1 Corinthians 16:22)
15. How many lions did Solomon have decorating the steps up to his throne? (1 Kings10:20)
16. What did John first see standing in heaven? (Revelation 5:6)
17. What are the first five books of the Old Testament called?
18. What swallowed the rebellious Korah? (Numbers 16:31-33)
19. What was Shadrach's Hebrew name? (Daniel 1:7)

20. What is bottomless in which the angel is from? (Revelation 9:11)

21. What word means reckons or is counted or is numbered? (Daniel 5:26)

22. What was the name of the blind beggar in Jericho who received sight from Jesus? (Mark 10:46-52)

```
L A S T Z X B R A N H C E S C
V A A C C U R S E D B N E W S
B N M P L K E J H F O U N D G
P S U B E H D H C E N S U S F
R A E Q C N W A E S R T Y U H
A V L N B M T N P T E N O T S
Y B A R T I M A E U S C I X Z
K R W H E D S N T S A M E N E
B Q E R M T M I N E S Y U I A
A P P Z P Z P A O R U N I N R
G E D A L I A H E X C C V B T
G N U L E J E V L E W T H E H
Y L A B I B L E S D F G A H J
I O P L N I S R A H P U N T K
Y T V I S I O N X F I N D O G
```

Puzzle 28

1. The name Moses means drawn out of what? (Exodus 2:10)

2. Daniel said the statue in Nebuchadnezzar's dream represented how many kingdoms? (Daniel 2:36-40)

3. Who was the daughter to Ahab and Jezebel? (2 Kings 8:18, 26)

4. Besides brass, what other metal did Tubal-cain work with? (Genesis 4:22)

5. When the voice from heaven said, "Blessed are the dead which die in the Lord from henceforth," they rest from their labors and what do their works do? (Revelation 14:13)

6. Before Jesus calmed the sea, where was he sleeping? (Mark 4:37-38)

7. Where did God tell Joseph to take Mary and baby Jesus to keep them safe? (Matthew 2:13)

8. What was Esther's Hebrew name? (Esther 2:7)

9. What word does "Ecclesiastes" mean? (Ecclesiastes 1:1)

10. Fill in the blank: "I am the Alpha and the Omega, the _____ and the End." (Revelation 21:6)

11. Isaiah 9:6 says that the Messiah is called the Prince of what? (Isaiah 9:6)

12. Whom did Paul accuse of being a hypocrite? (Galatians 2:11-14)

13. To what political party did Simon belong? (Luke 6:15)

14. What occupation did Huldah have? (2 Chronicles 34:22)

15. When the Israelites left Egypt, why did God keep them from going through the land of the Philistines? (Exodus 13:17)

16. Abaddon means "angel of the bottomless pit" in what language? (Revelation 9:11)

17. In the kingdom of God, the lion will lie down with what animal? (Isaiah 11:6)

18. What is another word for "hell"? (Psalm 16:10 NKJV)

19. What was red that parted as the people exited? (Exodus 13:18, 14:16-26)

20. What is the name for "angel of the bottomless pit" in Greek? (Revelation 9:11)

21. Who was the servant to Elah before he became king of Israel? (1 Kings 16:8–9)

22. After Queen Esther identified Haman as her enemy to King Xerxes, Haman tried to appeal to Esther and fell on what piece of furniture? (Esther 7:8)

Q	D	A	S	H	E	B	R	E	W	Z	X	C	V	Z
E	N	S	S	E	T	E	H	P	O	R	P	R	B	R
G	Z	I	M	R	I	M	A	F	L	O	T	A	L	H
P	E	E	T	R	E	G	V	H	L	A	J	B	K	C
Y	F	D	S	F	W	T	E	A	O	P	Q	B	W	A
T	Y	W	H	O	T	Z	A	B	F	O	R	E	R	E
U	I	H	A	U	S	O	E	W	H	L	Z	T	H	R
A	F	T	I	R	B	O	V	A	C	L	X	C	E	P
B	A	L	L	O	E	H	S	N	L	Y	U	M	A	L
W	I	Q	A	S	D	S	F	G	H	O	J	K	R	C
P	R	E	H	C	A	E	R	P	C	N	T	E	R	A
I	O	U	T	D	Y	A	G	A	I	N	T	N	T	L
P	N	Z	A	X	G	R	A	Y	C	E	V	A	B	V
M	N	H	A	N	O	I	N	T	P	E	A	C	E	E
B	E	G	I	N	N	I	N	G	L	T	J	H	G	S

Puzzle 29

1. Who did God assure that Israel would know God was with him just as He was with Moses? (Joshua 3:7)

2. At Lystra, the crowd was motivated to declare Paul and Barnabas as gods because Paul just healed what type of man? (Acts 14:8–12)

3. Which prophet brought a Shunammite's son back to life? (2 Kings 4:18–37)

4. What type men did Jesus ask, "Do you believe that I am able to do this?" (Matthew 9:28)

5. In Revelation 3:21, the church at Laodicea was told that if they overcame, they would be granted to do what with Him on His throne? (Revelation 3:21)

6. What was the name of the gate that Eliashib the High Priest and his priests built? (Nehemiah 3:1)

7. Who said this, "Silver and gold I have none"? (Acts 3:6)

8. Which wind blew away the locusts as one of the plagues on Egypt? (Exodus 10:19)

9. What major city was Bethany near? (John 11:18)

10. Fill in the blank: After landing at Fair Havens, Paul predicted a disastrous voyage if they continued, but the centurion followed the advice of the pilot and the _____ of the ship. (Acts 27:8–11)

11. When the disciples asked Jesus to tell them the signs of His coming and the end of the age, what prophet did Jesus quote? (Matthew 24:15)

12. How many cities were allotted to the priests in the Promised Land? (Joshua 21:19)

13. Besides Levi, what other son of Jacob slew all the males of Shechem's city in retaliation against that city's prince who raped their sister? (Genesis 34:25)

14. What part of the Passover lamb was to be put on the two side posts and the upper doorpost of each house? (Exodus 12:7)

15. Besides Mary, who else was also Lazarus's sister? (John 11:1)

16. By touching what part of the altar could someone claim sanctuary in the temple? (1 Kings 1:50–51)

17. Who did Samuel say would prophesy and be "turned into another man"? (1 Samuel 9:27; 10:6)

18. The Passover lamb was to be without what? (Exodus 12:5)

19. Who wrote "For by grace are ye saved through faith; and that not of yourselves: it is the gift of God: not of works, lest any man should boast"? (Ephesians 2:8–9)

20. Where was Moses when he cried out to the Lord because there was no water fit to drink? (Exodus 15:22)

21. How many mothers were there who together, bore Jacob twelve sons and one daughter? (Genesis 35:23–26)

22. Who took seven years to build the Lord's temple? (1 Kings 6:38)

```
H T N E E T M U X T T W E A K
E G G N E E T R I H T I Z X C
J K L J O S H U A A M N S B V
E P E T E R H D A W N S O U L
L A W W L R E S H D E F L G G
I U S U A L U Q T N O N O W N
S Y A T P P R S R U B Y M E O
H S U P I O E E A R Z F O U R
A B I V B C D E M L L X N Z T
A R T I C L E N H M E L K B S
C O H G I W O J H S I M E L B
R T O W N E R O F D N S T I O
O R R E W S Q A D I A M O N D
S T N E S T Y U I O D P T D Y
S B S I M E O N I C E V E R M
```

Puzzle 30

1. When the Israelites moved into the Promised Land, which city became the permanent home for the tabernacle? (Joshua 18:1)

2. Who set people with swords, spears, and bows in the lower and the higher places on the wall they were rebuilding? (Nehemiah 4:13)

3. Besides goat's hair, what other material was used to make the curtains for the tabernacle? (Exodus 26:1)

4. Which virgins did the five foolish virgins ask for oil for their lamps? (Matthew 25:8)

5. Who said, "The Lord gave, and the Lord hath taken away; blessed be the name of the Lord"? (Job 1:21)

6. During the ten plagues on Egypt, when the water turned to blood, what died? (Exodus 7:21)

7. Besides Nadab, what other son of Aaron was devoured by fire? (Leviticus 10:1–2)

8. What prophet got so angry at God that he told God to just go ahead and kill him? (Jonah 4:3)

9. For the Passover meal, the Israelites were to eat roasted lamb, unleavened bread, and what kind of herbs? (Exodus 12:8)

10. What judge of Israel had seventy sons? (Judges 8:30)

11. Who did God command to stretch out his rod so that the dust of the land would become lice? (Exodus 8:16)

12. Fill in the blank: The days are prolonged, and every _____ fails? (Ezekiel 12:22)

13. The Passover lamb was to be killed on which day of the month? (Exodus 12:6)

14. Who helped Zerubbabel rebuild the house of God again? (Ezra 5:2)

15. Luke journeyed with and recorded which famous missionary in the book of Acts? (Acts 1:1; 16:10)

16. Besides wisdom, what else did Solomon ask of God at the beginning of his reign? (1 Kings 3:9; 12)

17. What high priest did Paul call a whitewashed wall? (Acts 23:2–3)

18. Jesus told us to be of good cheer because He has overcome what? (John 16:33)

19. The name of what color sea did the locusts from the ten plagues on Egypt blow into? (Exodus 10:19)

20. Who was swallowed up by the earth, along with his fellow conspirators, because they had formed a rebellion against Moses and Aaron? (Numbers 16:32)

21. Who was Jesus asking, "Why are ye fearful, O ye of little faith?" (Matthew 8:25-26)

22. Which king asked Paul, "Do you think that in such a short time you can persuade me to be a Christian?" (Acts 26:28)

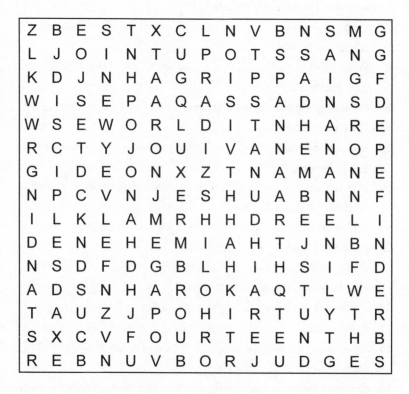

```
Z  B  E  S  T  X  C  L  N  V  B  N  S  M  G
L  J  O  I  N  T  U  P  O  T  S  S  A  N  G
K  D  J  N  H  A  G  R  I  P  P  A  I  G  F
W  I  S  E  P  A  Q  A  S  S  A  D  N  S  D
W  S  E  W  O  R  L  D  I  T  N  H  A  R  E
R  C  T  Y  J  O  U  I  V  A  N  E  N  O  P
G  I  D  E  O  N  X  Z  T  N  A  M  A  N  E
N  P  C  V  N  J  E  S  H  U  A  B  N  N  F
I  L  K  L  A  M  R  H  H  D  R  E  E  L  I
D  E  N  E  H  E  M  I  A  H  T  J  N  B  N
N  S  D  F  D  G  B  L  H  I  H  S  I  F  D
A  D  S  N  H  A  R  O  K  A  Q  T  L  W  E
T  A  U  Z  J  P  O  H  I  R  T  U  Y  T  R
S  X  C  V  F  O  U  R  T  E  E  N  T  H  B
R  E  B  N  U  V  B  O  R  J  U  D  G  E  S
```

Puzzle 31

1. What was the name of the father to two of Jesus' disciples, James and John? (Matthew 4:21)

2. Who rolled away the stone from Jesus' tomb on Easter morning and sat on it? (Matthew 28:2)

3. Who did Jesus gently rebuke for stressing out over hospitality details? (Luke 10:41)

4. According to Luke 3:5, what will be filled? (Luke 3:5)

5. Salvation belongs to whom? (Psalm 3:8)

6. Who helped Jeshua rebuild the temple when the Israelites returned from Babylon? (Ezra 5:2)

7. Who was writing to say he was sending the slave back home? (Philemon 1:1, 12)

8. What word, similar to Sibboleth, was used to trap the Ephraimites? (Judges 12:4-6)

9. What king made a detailed organization of temple personnel? (1 Chronicles 23:6)

10. In the Old Testament, what evil king had a wife who was just as evil as he was? (1 Kings 19:1-2)

11. Difficult is the way and what is the gate which leadeth unto life? (Matthew 7:14 NKJV)

12. What was the name of the river that John the Baptist baptized people in? (Mark 1:5)

13. Fill in the blank: "But he that entereth in by the _____ is the shepherd of the sheep." (John 10:2)

14. In what city did Jesus raise the son of a widow from the dead? (Luke 7:11-15)

15. What poisonous animal bit Paul but he had no harm come to him? (Acts 28:3-5)

16. To whom did Jesus say, "Get thee behind me, Satan?" (Matthew 16:23)

17. How many stars were in the garland on the woman's head? (Revelation 12:1)

18. According to the book of Numbers, a Star (meaning the Messiah) shall come out of what? (Numbers 24:17)

19. Which king was Isaiah speaking to when he gave the sign of the virgin birth? (Isaiah 7:10–14)

20. From where will we hear a voice say, "This is the way, walk ye in it"? (Isaiah 30:21)

21. Who was the last person on earth to see the ark of the covenant? (Revelation 11:19)

22. What was the original name of Benjamin, Jacob's son? (Genesis 35:18)

```
F  Z  T  X  M  O  N  E  Y  C  V  B  L  L  N
R  A  I  N  A  I  N  T  E  N  S  E  U  A  M
O  L  N  K  R  H  J  R  H  G  T  R  A  C  E
N  S  Y  O  T  R  A  I  N  W  D  F  P  E  A
T  A  O  Q  H  W  E  B  E  N  O  N  I  L  R
Z  D  P  L  A  R  K  L  O  I  U  R  Y  E  T
R  I  V  E  R  X  V  H  C  D  V  J  R  B  N
B  V  A  L  L  E  Y  G  N  M  B  O  C  A  J
L  A  K  N  J  H  G  I  T  S  F  R  D  B  N
F  D  K  J  G  A  H  H  O  U  N  D  Z  B  S
L  O  W  Q  W  E  E  R  O  R  S  A  T  U  Y
S  H  I  B  B  O  L  E  T  H  H  N  K  R  U
I  I  G  O  P  L  O  T  K  A  E  J  H  E  G
D  G  L  I  O  N  R  E  E  D  E  B  E  Z  F
N  H  O  J  S  Z  D  P  I  E  R  X  C  V  B
```

Puzzle 32

1. How many sons did Abraham have with Keturah? (Genesis 25:1–2)

2. What prophet said the Israelites "enter at the windows like a thief"? (Joel 2:9)

3. A proverb says that whoever is a partner with a thief hates his own what? (Proverbs 29:24 NKJV)

4. Who killed two people with one spear? (Numbers 25:7–8)

5. Which of the tribes established its own idolatrous calf? (Judges 18:30)

6. Besides David, what other king also wrote psalms? (Psalm 72)

7. The Lord is my what and my salvation? (Psalm 27:1)

8. What Old Testament prophet saw a flying scroll? (Zechariah 5:1)

9. The people of what island said that Paul was a god because a poisonous snake bite didn't harm him? (Acts 28:6 NKJV)

10. Who prophesied with a harp? (1 Chronicles 25:3)

11. The parable of the lost sheep can be found in Matthew and what other book of the Bible? (Luke 15:4–7)

12. How many men did Moses send to explore the Promised Land? (Numbers 13:1–14)

13. Who was the servant to the prophet Elisha? (2 Kings 5:20)

14. Fill in the blank: Jesus said, "My sheep hear my voice, and I know them, and they _____ me." (John 10:27)

15. Who saw the river of the water of life in the new heaven? (Revelation 22:1)

16. In which direction was the star located that the magi were following? (Matthew 2:2)

17. The altar in the tabernacle was overlaid with what material? (Exodus 27:2)

18. When the scribes and Pharisees demanded a sign from Jesus, what sign did He give them? (Matthew 12:39–41 NIV)

19. What army of people were the Israelites battling on the day the sun stood still? (Joshua 10:12–14)

20. What item did Jeremiah see marred at the potter's place? (Jeremiah 18:4)

21. Who was David's oldest brother? (1 Samuel 17:28)

22. How many curtains did the tabernacle have? (Exodus 26:1)

```
B A B E L I A B O O N A M E S
Z X C V U B N P N M L K A J H
T R U C K S R U H G D A L E S
W S D Z E C H A R I A H T H K
E V L E W T F L Q W N E A R T
L C I V U B N S M C R E A S T
E X F D Z D F A I N T A H S D
V S E J T O P S I X H G E A F
E J O E L O K H L L P T O R S
W E R L T G E H A Z I Y U B I
Q Z O E O X C U V R B G N N M
F W D S G M H M O V E J H K L
O A W S E A O M F Y T O O T H
L J K E M H A N O J J M L E P
L O W V X C A M P E R E I N S
```

Puzzle 33

1. Fill in the blank: In Revelation 1:8, Jesus says He is the _____ and the Omega, the beginning and the end. (Revelation 1:8)

2. What word means "resting"? (Genesis 2:2)

3. Jesus said He came not to destroy the Law but to do what with it? (Matthew 5:17)

4. What judge's other name was Jerubbaal? (Judges 7:1)

5. How many of the ten lepers whom Jesus cleansed came back to thank Him? (Luke 17:12–16)

6. The angels told the shepherds that the sign unto to them would be a babe lying in what? (Luke 2:12)

7. John described the Lamb he saw in heaven as having seven horns and seven of what else? (Revelation 5:6)

8. When Moses blessed the tribes before his death, which tribe did he say dwelt like a lion? (Deuteronomy 33:20)

9. Peter said what was "incorruptible, and undefiled, and that fadeth not away, reserved in heaven for you"? (1 Peter 1:3–4)

10. Who was the sleepy young man that fell from an upper window and died during a sermon by the apostle Paul? (Acts 20:9–12)

11. God gave Moses the Ten Commandments on the name of what mountain? (Exodus 19:18)

12. What king refused to tell his astrologers his dream so they could interpret it? (Daniel 2:1–9)

13. Better is a neighbor nearby than what far away? (Proverbs 27:10)

14. Who was a deaconess in the New Testament? (Romans 16:1 NIV)

15. What name means "seen God's face"? (Genesis 32:30)

16. Who purposed in his heart that he would not defile himself? (Daniel 1:8)

17. How many shekels of silver did Joseph's brothers sell him for? (Genesis 37:28)

18. Who stretched his hand over the sea to divide the waters? (Exodus 14:21)

19. What was Jacob's name changed to? (Genesis 32:28)
20. Herodias was the wife to what king when she engineered the execution of John the Baptist? (Mark 6:14, 21-25)
21. Jesus told the disciples to rejoice because their names are written where? (Luke 10:20)
22. Samuel said "To obey is better than sacrifice" to whom? (1 Samuel 15:22-24)

```
Z X P E N I E L C O R N E R C
K S E S O M E L B M N A B E V
P L A I S A B B A T H J L A E
A P S U R N D F L P G E H L Y
A Q H S L G F U L F I L L T E
L Y I O T E R A S N E W N Y S
P I N H E R I T A N C E C U I
H W S X U B Z D A S W Q H P O
H B R O T H E R E T I D A C H
A T I N Y T R G A D F N L E V
Y H N M C L L A M A O J A U D
T E E C H O L G K E I V K I O
R N E B U C H A D N E Z Z A R
O P T I S O N I Z N X C V B E
T M A P P N G N I N N U R X H
```

Puzzle 34

1. Fill in the blank: Cursed is the one who moves his neighbor's _____ . (Deuteronomy 27:17)

2. What disciple was also known as Levi? (Matthew 9:9; Mark 2:14)

3. Who killed all her grandchildren so she could be queen? (2 Kings 11:1)

4. Paul said when our earthly tent is destroyed, God gives us what that is not made with hands, "eternal in the heavens"? (2 Corinthians 5:1)

5. What was the name of Ruth and Boaz's son? (Ruth 4:17)

6. Peter said Christ is a lamb without spot or what else? (1 Peter 1:19)

7. Where were the Israelites when God sent the manna? (Exodus 16:3)

8. What occupation did Abel, Rachel, and Zipporah have in common? (Genesis 4:2; 29:9; Exodus 2:16, 21)

9. When God tested Abraham, He told Abraham to take Isaac up what mountain? (Genesis 22:1-2)

10. The Hebrew word *Abaddon* is translated into *Apollyon* in what language? (Revelation 9:11)

11. In Revelation, Jesus is described as the Lion of what tribe? (Revelation 5:5)

12. In Nebuchadnezzar's dream image, what part of the image was made out of iron and clay? (Daniel 2:33)

13. Besides silver, gold, flocks, and herds, what else did the Israelites have when they left Egypt? (Exodus 12:35 NIV)

14. Who did Queen Esther identify as her enemy to King Xerxes/Ahasuerus? (Esther 7:6)

15. Paul said that when the Lord comes, He will bring to light what things in the darkness? (1 Corinthians 4:5)

16. What word means "accursed"? (1 Corinthians 16:22)

17. Elijah called down fire from heaven to defeat the prophets of Baal on what mountain? (1 Kings 18:19)

18. What were James and John doing with their nets when Jesus called them to follow Him? (Matthew 4:21)

19. Who cursed the day he was born? (Job 3:1)

20. Herod ordered all the children in Bethlehem from what age and younger to be killed? (Matthew 2:16)

21. Besides Ephesians, Paul wrote what other epistle telling children to obey their parents? (Colossians 3:20)

22. What field was purchased using the thirty pieces of silver after Judas threw them back at the Pharisees? (Matthew 27:7)

```
M N B V B O O K L C X S N E A
G D S F M O R I A H Z E A Z T
N F G S E A T T R A D E H J G
I H S I M E L B K D C R E B N
H A Y D U I T E I O P L S K I
T M N S D R E H P E H S S T D
O A C X Z R J Q W A E R E G L
L N N V G B N U I M P I N T I
C N C A R M E L D S T I R L U
B I K J T R A C E A D E E D B
I A W Q A H S D D N H F D G H
B M A T T H E W E D A I L Y E
L V C A W B X M Z P G Y I T R
E C O L O S S I A N S A W X B
S M N J U G G L E R E T T O P
```

Puzzle 35

1. Who said, "Let us also go, that we may die with him" when he learned that Jesus was going to the home of Lazarus? (John 11:16)

2. On what mountain did Solomon build the temple? (2 Chronicles 3:1)

3. What did Samuel tell the Israelites to prepare for the Lord? (1 Samuel 7:3)

4. Whose sons were consumed by fire for offering an unholy sacrifice in the tabernacle? (Leviticus 10:1)

5. Where were their shoes when the Israelites were commanded to eat with their staffs in their hands while the tenth plague descended upon Egypt? (Exodus 12:11)

6. Who immediately refused to eat unclean food upon being brought captive to Babylonian? (Daniel 1:8)

7. Who was Noah's great-grandfather? (Genesis 5:22–29)

8. Fill in the blank: According to James, the effective prayers of a _____ man "availeth much"? (James 5:16)

9. What king was condemned for acting as a priest? (1 Samuel 13:8–14)

10. What was the short outer garment priests wore over their robes? (Exodus 28:6–14)

11. What Pharisee came to see Jesus at night? (John 3:1–2)

12. How did the believers react to Paul when he returned to Jerusalem after his conversion? (Acts 9:26)

13. What prophet did God command to lie on his left side for three hundred and ninety days? (Ezekiel 4:4–5)

14. Who said, "Ye exact usury, every one of his brother"? (Nehemiah 5:7)

15. In Revelation 3:21, the church at Laodicea was told that if they did overcame, they would be granted to sit with Him where? (Revelation 3:21)

16. Which of David's sons was overly proud of his physical beauty? (2 Samuel 14:25–27)

17. God commanded Moses to take a handful of what from the furnace and scatter to cause boils on the Egyptians? (Exodus 9:8-9)

18. Who said, "Am I my brother's keeper?" (Genesis 4:9)

19. Besides Hanani, who else did Nehemiah assign to be in charge of opening and closing the gates of Jerusalem and guarding the city? (Nehemiah 7:2-3)

20. The Roman commander called for soldiers, horsemen, and spearmen to safely take Paul to what governor in the city of Caesarea? (Acts 23:23-24)

21. Who was Jesus asking, "Who do people say that I am?" (Matthew 16:13)

22. What prophet helped anoint King Solomon? (1 Kings 1:34)

```
C D I S C I P L E S Z X C V A
R A F G H J K L A M S N B L F
E N I C O D E M U S D A E S R
A Y T N R O O E O W Q I U A I
T L U I O H Q S I L K A Z L A
X F E E T P W T R E A T S X D
I E E I D E N H Z A S S A R B
L B N G N N T E R K U F B V C
E M O R I A H A H O R S E A P
F N C H Y U D R E E J M K A I
A S H E S I N T B V M C X R Z
C M L K A J H S H G F I S O B
E T D R I G H T N A T H A N D
S A F Q I W E R T E N O R H T
X A Y R H A N A N I A H U B Z
```

Puzzle 36

1. Who said we are not to think of ourselves more highly than we ought? (Romans 12:3)
2. Who co-conspired with Geshem to trick Nehemiah into leaving his work and come meet with them? (Nehemiah 6:2–3)
3. After landing at Fair Havens, Paul predicted a disastrous voyage if they continued, but who followed the advice of the pilot and the owner of the ship instead? (Acts 27:8–11)
4. What famous spy was the uncle of Othniel? (Judges 3:9)
5. Who was the first prophet in the Bible? (Numbers 12:6–8)
6. What blew in on the east wind to deeply annoy Egypt during the time of the ten plagues? (Exodus 10:13)
7. What high priest anointed Solomon as king? (1 Kings 1:39)
8. In Revelation 2:7, the church at Ephesus was told that if they overcame, they would be given to eat from the what of life? (Revelation 2:7)
9. Who secretly hid stolen plunder in the ground under his tent? (Joshua 7:20–21)
10. Who did Jesus ask, "Could you not watch with Me one hour?" (Matthew 26:40)
11. When Jesus preached, "Woe unto you, scribes and Pharisees, hypocrites," he used a camel and what insect to illustrate His point? (Matthew 23:23–24)
12. Who was the sorcerer at Paphos who was struck blind by Paul for his heresy? (Acts 13:8)
13. Twelve of what item was used to make the memorial for the Jordan River crossing? (Joshua 4:3)
14. The Lord prepares for us a table in the presence of whom? (Psalm 23:5)
15. What prophet did God command to marry an unfaithful wife? (Hosea 1:2)

16. On the first Passover, it was commanded that "this day shall be unto you for what"? (Exodus 12:14)

17. Moses and Aaron were denied entrance into the Promised Land because of an act of impatience and faithlessness at where? (Numbers 20:12-13)

18. Who was the godly son born to Hannah and Elkanah in answer to prayer? (1 Samuel 1:19-20)

19. Besides praying and laying their hands on Paul and Barnabas before sending them apart for missionary service, what else did the church at Antioch do? (Acts 13:3)

20. Who said, "If thou be the Son of God, command that these stones be made bread"? (Matthew 4:3)

21. To what priestly division did Zechariah belong? (Luke 1:5 NIV)

22. How many kings did Isaiah serve as a prophet? (Isaiah 1:1)

```
P O Y T R E D E T S A F E T Y
G Q P A U L W E H R T Y B E H
A V E C X Z O A S A M U E L O
N A T A S B J C N M B E L L S
T D E F G I H J U K L P A C E
S A R G B E T T R S H S C Q A
W D S A N B A L L A T W A S R
E R T F Y A P N B L Z S A Y N
Z A D O K Q T I R A C E R S A
W S X U C D R E R I F N V T H
B T A R C E N T U R I O N E C
G R T M M P R A Y O Y T U M A
O A I K Y S E S O M R S M J S
L S B I B L I C A E L P Z X H
C H I L D R E N E M I E S W E
```

Puzzle 37

1. What was the name of the great star that fell in Revelation? (Revelation 8:10–11)

2. What group of people did many signs and wonders in the New Testament? (Acts 2:43)

3. What New Testament book of the Bible is specifically addressed to the twelve tribes? (James 1:1)

4. In the Sermon of the Mount, Jesus spoke about laying up treasure where because it would be safe from thieves? (Matthew 6:19–20)

5. Who was Leah's maidservant? (Genesis 29:24)

6. Jesus said if we believe in Him, then out of what will flow rivers of living water? (John 7:38 NKJV)

7. The tribes Reuben, Gad, and the half tribe of Maasseh settled on the east side of which river? (Joshua 18:7)

8. What was Ezekiel told to do with the scroll filled with lament, mourning, and woe? (Ezekiel 2:10–3:1)

9. When Jacob was blessing his sons, which son did he say was like a serpent and a viper? (Genesis 49:17)

10. For one judgment, Jesus said that all the nations will be gathered before Him, and the people will be separated like sheep from what other animal? (Matthew 25:33)

11. Which of his brothers did Absalom kill to avenge Tamar's honor? (2 Samuel 13:28–29)

12. What type of oil was to be used for the lamp in the tabernacle? (Exodus 27:20)

13. Zeruiah and Abigail were the sisters to which famous king? (1 Chronicles 2:13–16)

14. Who did God command to bake cakes using human waste as fuel and then eat these cakes? (Ezekiel 4:12)

15. What type of animals did God shut the mouths of when Daniel was condemned to spend the night with them? (Daniel 6:22)

16. Who said, "My eyes have seen your salvation"? (Luke 2:25–30)

17. How many sons did Ishmael have? (Genesis 17:20)
18. The Lord told Ananias that what man was His chosen vessel? (Acts 9:10–11)
19. Besides Revelation, what other book of the Bible describes Michael fighting with Satan? (Jude 1:9)
20. Job said that He knows the way that I take; when He has tested me, I shall come forth as what? (Job 23:10)
21. What brave woman used a tent stake peg to kill one of Israel's enemies? (Judges 4:21)
22. Who sent twelve men up a mountain to check out the Promised Land? (Numbers 13:17)

```
M J A R N T R Y B K E E S V C
V A S T A O G I D D Y E A T X
Z M A S D P M O S E S T U F T
H E A R T K O Z H V E I L G L
L S P O I W U S T E P S L E Y
X Z Q A M N O N T R W E I R T
C P A R K I N G V L B K O N M
J T O K C O A R S E E L N O D
H W Z X A G D A F Z A S S W E
T E S I M E O N E D R F I N D
S L A V L E O L I V E Y U E P
T V X E E P C V D B N M O V I
A E R D A N A D R O J Z D A N
M P L U J D K H J G F S D E A
P O Y J U G T R E W P Q E H S
```

Puzzle 38

1. Whom did God choose as the master craftsman who would build the tabernacle? (Exodus 31:1–2)

2. In the valley showed to him by the Lord, as Ezekiel prophesied, what sound was heard as all the dry bones came together? (Ezekiel 37:7 NKJV)

3. According to the Psalms, what has God removed from us as far as the east is from west? (Psalm 103:12)

4. Whose army fought with pitchers and torches? (Judges 7:19–20)

5. According to Peter, we are to stand steadfast in what in order to resist Satan? (1 Peter 5:9)

6. Against which tribe did the children of Israel wage war for evil done to the concubine of a Levite? (Judges 20:4–17)

7. Fill in the blank: Peter said we were like sheep gone astray, but now we are returned to the Shepherd and Overseer of our _____ . (1 Peter 2:25)

8. To whom did Jesus say, "Today salvation has come to this house"? (Luke 19:8–9)

9. According to the Proverbs, he who speaks what declares righteousness? (Proverbs 12:17)

10. Who was to serve the people of Israel as a watchman? (Ezekiel 3:17)

11. The spies went into the land of Canaan from which direction? (Numbers 13:22)

12. In the Great Commission, Jesus says that those who believe in Him will take up what type of animals? (Mark 16:18)

13. What book of the Bible contains the verse where Jesus says He is the Bright and Morning Star? (Revelation 22:16)

14. What king of Israel started out good and then let his wives lead him into worship of Ashtoreth and other false gods? (1 Kings 11:4–5)

15. Barabbas, whom the people chose instead of Jesus, was what sort of person? (John 18:40)

16. Who was told that the Valley of Hinnom would come to be called the valley of slaughter? (Jeremiah 7:32)

17. What did Paul say we have in earthen vessels? (2 Corinthians 4:7)

18. Fill in the blank: "And You give them drink from the _____ of Your pleasures." (Psalm 36:8 NKJV)

19. Who was Rachel's maidservant? (Genesis 30:2–3)

20. According to the proverbs, what sort of son makes a glad father? (Proverbs 10:1)

21. What famous ancestor did the Moabites and the Ammonites have in common? (Genesis 19:30, 36–38)

22. Who was Abram's sister? (Genesis 20:2, 11–12)

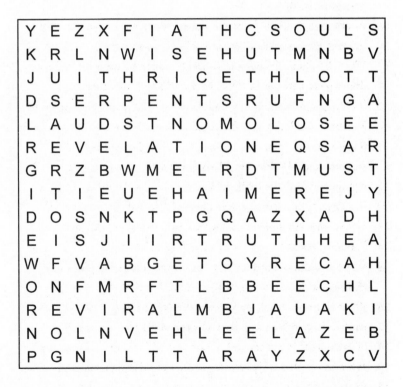

```
Y E Z X F I A T H C S O U L S
K R L N W I S E H U T M N B V
J U I T H R I C E T H L O T T
D S E R P E N T S R U F N G A
L A U D S T N O M O L O S E E
R E V E L A T I O N E Q S A R
G R Z B W M E L R D T M U S T
I T I E U E H A I M E R E J Y
D O S N K T P G Q A Z X A D H
E I S J I I R T R U T H H E A
W F V A B G E T O Y R E C A H
O N F M R F T L B B E E C H L
R E V I R A L M B J A U A K I
N O L N V E H L E E L A Z E B
P G N I L T T A R A Y Z X C V
```

Puzzle 39

1. In Micah 6:8, we are to do justly, walk humbly with God, and love what? (Micah 6:8)

2. Who was the silversmith who made shrines to the goddess Diana for a living? (Acts 19:24)

3. How many lions did Solomon have decorating his throne? (1 Kings 10:19)

4. What does "Anakim" mean? (Deuteronomy 2:11)

5. To whom was God speaking when He said, "Say unto the children of Israel, I AM hath sent me unto you." (Exodus 3:14)

6. Mount Calvary is also called Golgotha, which means what? (Matthew 27:33)

7. What does "Bethel" mean? (Genesis 28:17)

8. What occupation did Festus have? (Acts 24:10, 27)

9. The Festival of Unleavened Bread is known by what other name? (Exodus 12:11, 17)

10. Who made an oath in the New Testament to give someone up to half his kingdom? (Mark 6:21, 23)

11. Rather than seeking food, drink, and clothing, what of God's should believers seek first? (Matthew 6:31, 33)

12. When the Israelites left Egypt, whose land did God keep them from going through because of war? (Exodus 13:17)

13. What were the magi following? (Matthew 2:2)

14. The Lord hates what type of way? (Psalm 119:104)

15. What is another word for "the lot" during Queen Esther's day? (Esther 9:24)

16. What was Hananiah's Babylonian name? (Daniel 1:7)

17. James said we are to be doers of the word, not just what? (James 1:22)

18. Who was cursed with sorrow in conception and childbirth? (Genesis 3:16)

19. In Revelation, the tabernacle of God is with who and He will dwell with them, and be their God? (Revelation 21:3)

20. Who was the wife of Chuza, Herod's servant? (Luke 8:3)
21. King Uzziah was stricken with leprosy because he was burning what in the temple? (2 Chronicles 26:19)
22. In Nebuchadnezzar's dream image, what was the head made out of? (Daniel 2:32)

```
R O N R E V O G Y M H O E S Q
O P E N T W E E T C R A F T H
E Z X C T V B N A M R S L K O
S S P A G H E R T I T E H J U
L L U K S T D G P N F R M D C
A Y T O R A E W A Q A A S N E
F L A P H I L I S T I N E S M
H U I S A L G O S I X M Z O E
E E N B A N N A O J V C D X L
A M A S E R V E V L K G O L D
R E A R S S D F E G N H R J S
T A U D E M E T R I U S E P N
S P K S Q R W V K E K R H E O
U Y O T R E S N E C N I T R S
I M O V I N G P K I N G D M V
```

PUZZLE 40

1. Who was the key character for being a good neighbor in Jesus' parable to answer the question, "Who is my neighbor?" (Luke 10:33)

2. What item of the king's was gold that he extended to visitors so they wouldn't get the death sentence? (Esther 4:11)

3. Who was a servant of King Saul? (1 Samuel 21:7)

4. Isaiah prophesied that the Messiah would be led as a lamb to the what? (Isaiah 53:7)

5. Who swore an oath that he didn't know Jesus? (Matthew 26:69, 72)

6. Besides saying "peace," what else did Jesus say to calm the sea? (Mark 4:39)

7. What shepherd became one of God's prophets? (Amos 1:1)

8. What was Miriam stricken with for speaking against Moses' wife? (Numbers 12:10)

9. What was the name of Timothy's grandmother? (2 Timothy 1:5)

10. *Boanerges* meant what? (Mark 3:17)

11. What minor prophet prophesied about the outpouring of God's Spirit at Pentecost? (Joel 2:28–29)

12. What occupation did Anna of the New Testament have? (Luke 2:36)

13. Besides Moses, who else did Korah lead a revolt against? (Numbers 16:20–21)

14. Who broke a Nazarite vow which caused his death? (Judges 16:17)

15. How many queens are mentioned in the book of Esther? (Esther 1:9; 2:22)

16. What was Daniel's Babylonian name? (Daniel 1:7)

17. Shimei cursed King David during Absalom's rebellion by throwing what at him? (2 Samuel 16:6, 13 NIV)

18. What do the seven lampstands in Revelation 1:20 represent? (Revelation 1:20)

19. Peter said Christ is a lamb without blemish and without what else? (1 Peter 1:19)
20. Who called the Lord "Thou God seest me"? (Genesis 16:8, 13)
21. *Abaddon* and *Apollyon* both mean what creature of the bottomless pit? (Revelation 9:11)
22. What tribe did the apostle Paul hail from? (Philippians 3:5)

```
R Z S E H C R U H C A T D O G
E N B A R R I V E V C X W J S
D M S A M A R I T A N S L O K
N Q A C S D T F G L H M E J
U N D U E W O E H A G A R L R
H X Z A Q P Y N U P O I U Y T
T S W E S S T G D C V F R N T
P O P R O P H E T E S S I O R
P O O R N T B G R O O M O R E
E H P B E L T E S H A Z Z A R
E E E R Y U J L M J K L I A T
L Z T G P D L A N E E O L O P
O X E U N I C E C G R I U P E
R O R B T R B A N D U S E V C
D N M S L T R A Y E L L O W S
```

Puzzle 41

1. Jesus healed on what day which angered the Pharisees? (John 9:14-16)

2. Uzzah died from accidentally touching what? (2 Samuel 6:67)

3. Who said, "Lord, if it is You, command me to come to You"? (Matthew 14:28)

4. In Revelation 2:11, the church at Smyrna was told that if they overcame, they would not be hurt by what type of death? (Revelation 2:11)

5. What priest also served as a scribe, documenting the return of the Babylonian captives to Jerusalem? (Ezra 7:11)

6. What plague lasted three days and covered the land? (Exodus 10:22)

7. Of what country did Obadiah prophesy? (Obadiah 1:1)

8. Who was the king of Persia who made the proclaimation to allow God's people to return to Jerusalem? (Ezra 1:1)

9. What prophet had a live coal put in his mouth? (Isaiah 6:6-7)

10. What type of plant was to be dipped in the blood to put the blood on the doorsteps? (Exodus 12:22)

11. By pride comes nothing but what? (Proverbs 13:10 NKJV)

12. What priest allowed David to eat the shewbread? (1 Samuel 21:1, 6)

13. For the Passover meal, the Israelites were to eat roasted lamb, bitter herbs, and what kind of bread? (Exodus 12:8)

14. Who was Jethro's son-in-law? (Exodus 18:12)

15. To whom was God speaking when He asked, "Where were you when I laid the foundations of the earth?" (Job 38:1, 4)

16. Where will the ark of the covenant ultimately be found? (Revelation 11:19)

17. Who requested wisdom and understanding from the Lord at the beginning of his reign? (1 Kings 3:9-12)

18. John said what can overcome the world? (1 John 5:4)

19. Besides Joseph, who else was Jesus asking, "Did you not know that I must be about My Father's business? (Luke 2:41, 49)

20. How many sons of the priest Sceva were trying to cast out evil spirits? (Acts 19:13-16)
21. Who unknowingly offered to sacrifice his daughter to God? (Judges 11:30-34)
22. The people of which city were motivated to worship Paul and Barnabas as gods? (Acts 14:8-13)

```
P E O Y R A M A N E I U Y S H
D D A S A U Q W N Z E J R T T
S O L O M O N E A R R O A R S
E M F O G H V L J A K B L I A
C Z S X C A V B E N B M S F B
O E Q J E P H T H A H A E E B
S W H H E L O S S V X V Z B B
N E P A T A P E D C A E E V A
D E E D I T O R T R A I N F T
M A T X A A S Y T E N D H E H
J G E M F N S S S E N K R A D
C Y R U S U Y I T O T E I R O
V R C X Z L H P C A N L I K L
B O N A H I M E L E C H M L K
H S J D E N S E A V A E L N N
```

Puzzle 42

1. What king had seven hundred wives? (1 Kings 11:1–3)

2. What king was Mephibosheth's grandfather? (2 Samuel 9:6)

3. Besides the birds and the sun, what other hazard befell the seeds in Jesus' parable of the sower? (Matthew 13:4–7)

4. Who did Jesus ask, "What is your name?" (Luke 8:30)

5. The king of Persia brought forth what items of the house of the Lord that Nebuchadnezzar had brought forth out of Jerusalem? (Ezra 1:7)

6. Besides Priscilla, who else was a tentmaker who offered hospitality to Paul in Corinth? (Acts 18:2–3)

7. How many tribes of Israel went back to Jerusalem after their Babylonian captivity? (Ezra 1:5)

8. What false prophet prophesied against Jeremiah and died? (Jeremiah 28:15–17)

9. In Revelation 2:26, the church at Thyatira was told that if they overcame, they would be given what over nations? (Revelation 2:26)

10. What false prophets did Elijah defeat on Mount Carmel when fire fell from heaven? (1 Kings 18:19)

11. On what article of the high priest's clothing were the Urim and Thummim placed? (Leviticus 8:8)

12. Fill in the blank: While praying in the temple, Paul had a vision in which the Lord said, "Depart, for I will send thee far hence unto the _____"? (Acts 22:21)

13. What son was given to Adam and Eve to replace Abel? (Genesis 4:25)

14. What priest during the reign of King Ahaz built an altar based on the design of an altar in Damascus? (2 Kings 16:11)

15. How many wise virgins were there in Jesus' parable of the foolish and wise virgins? (Matthew 25:2)

16. Who did God ask, "Where are you?" (Genesis 3:9)

17. Where did God command Moses to take the ashes from in order to scatter them to cause boils on the Egyptians? (Exodus 9:8–9)

18. What was the name of Jeremiah's scribe? (Jeremiah 36:4)

19. How many days was the Feast of the Unleavened bread commanded to last? (Exodus 12:15)

20. What New Testament person said, "Whatever you ask me, I will give you, up to half my kingdom"? (Mark 6:22)

21. God told Joshua that Israel would know that God was with him just as He was with who? (Joshua 3:7)

22. Where was Paul when he was near death and urged Timothy to come before winter? (2 Timothy 1:16; 2:9)

```
R E C E I V E Z X C V B N N M
E G H V R A I N S A L E J K L
V F D I B S A H Q A V A W E S
I E Y F U R N A C E U T A R U
V U S I O P E N S Z A L Q B N
E V F S R E D A C X I S S W O
T H R E E B G N S U S E T H S
H U J L M L N I Q T H Y E T I
O I W I L L S A K L P O W E R
R K L T M N B H V C X L Z P P
N J H N G B A R U C H F A S T
S E W E Q J E S T A E S E T D
O L E G I O N R T Y R S U I E
M V C R X N O M O L O S Z P O
E S U R R E A D A M D A W N X
```

Puzzle 43

1. When the twelve men were sent to check out the Promised Land, what kind of fruit was so big that it took two men to carry one cluster on a pole between them? (Numbers 13:23)

2. Who was Laban's sister? (Genesis 24:29)

3. On what day of creation did God create the stars? (Genesis 1:16–19)

4. Samson's story is found in what book of the Bible? (Judges 13–16)

5. On what day did God bless and sanctify, and later called it Sabbath day, because creation was completed and God rested on that day? (Genesis 2:3)

6. How many sons did the father have in the parable of the prodigal son? (Luke 15:11)

7. What was the name of the servant whom Abraham was going to make his heir before Isaac was born? (Genesis 15:2)

8. Where were the Israelites when they were bitten by snakes? (Numbers 21:5–6)

9. On what item did the words "Mene, Mene, Tekel, Upharsin" come to appear in King Belshazzar's palace? (Daniel 5:5, 25)

10. What famous leader of Israel married an Ethiopian woman? (Numbers 12:1)

11. Matthew says that the criminals crucified with Christ were what? (Matthew 27:44)

12. In what city did the tabernacle stay once the Israelites settled in the Promised Land? (Joshua 18:1)

13. When we do what with our sins, God then forgives us of our sins and cleanses us from all unrighteousness? (1 John 1:9)

14. In Revelation, the Lord God told John that He was the Alpha and the what? (Revelation 1:8)

15. What Old Testament person believed in the Lord and it was counted to him for righteousness? (Genesis 15:1, 6)

16. Fill in the blank: "Your princes are rebellious, and _____ of thieves." (Isaiah 1:23 NKJV)

17. What was the name of Aaron's wife? (Exodus 6:23)

18. According to James, what will Satan do if we resist him? (James 4:7)

19. The tribe of Benjamin was famous for using which of their hands predominantly? (Judges 20:15-16)

20. What did Moses have to keep raised in order for the Israelites to prevail in battle? (Exodus 17:8-16)

21. According to the Psalms, who prepares a table before me in the presence of my enemies? (Psalm 23:1, 5)

22. Jesus said they would be dashed to what like the potter's vessels? (Revelation 2:27)

```
W  I  R  L  M  A  R  B  A  D  E  S  R  N  E
I  L  E  T  M  A  T  O  E  O  M  E  G  A  S
L  Q  Z  X  C  A  H  E  A  D  V  P  H  B  L
D  W  E  L  E  L  I  S  H  E  B  A  M  N  O
S  H  I  L  O  H  E  K  E  J  K  R  H  S  R
S  I  L  L  X  E  V  E  R  E  I  G  N  O  D
E  G  E  F  D  D  E  S  B  A  M  O  S  E  S
F  G  R  A  B  E  S  E  R  E  I  W  E  Q  T
N  T  Y  H  O  U  R  U  I  N  O  P  G  Z  W
O  Q  S  T  O  E  W  N  A  H  A  N  D  S  U
C  W  S  N  C  C  O  P  E  X  C  W  U  D  O
T  R  E  E  N  E  M  I  E  S  A  V  J  O  S
U  F  E  V  B  O  G  V  T  L  S  Y  W  H  N
R  L  S  E  C  E  I  P  L  E  F  T  O  R  N
F  N  M  S  J  U  I  K  F  O  U  R  T  H  L
```

Puzzle 44

1. Which tribe was often identified as a "half tribe"? (Deuteronomy 3:13)

2. How many loaves of the shewbread were to be on the table in the tabernacle Sabbath after Sabbath? (Leviticus 24:5)

3. According to the Psalms, how long will we dwell in the House of the Lord? (Psalm 23:6)

4. Gehazi was the servant of what prophet? (2 Kings 5:20)

5. True or false: God assigned the sea a limit. (Proverbs 8:29)

6. Which of Jacob's sons had twin sons born to him? (Genesis 38:26–30)

7. Fill in the blank: James said, "The effective, fervent prayer of a righteous man _____ much." (James 5:16 NKJV)

8. Who was Keturah's husband? (Genesis 25:1)

9. What animal did Samson kill with his bare hands? (Judges 14:5–6)

10. As Jesus hung on the cross, the two thieves originally did what to Him? (Mark 15:32)

11. If the slave owed money to Philemon, who said they would repay that debt? (Philemon 1:18–19)

12. John the Baptist called the Pharisees and Sadducees a generation of what type animal? (Matthew 3:7)

13. In Revelation, which of the four horses is the one whose rider represents death? (Revelation 6:8)

14. How many deacons were selected in Acts 6? (Acts 6:3)

15. When God spoke to the Israelites on Mount Sinai, one of the Ten Commandments was to remember which day in particular and to keep it holy? (Exodus 20:8)

16. What judge of Israel used an ox goad to kill his enemies? (Judges 3:31)

17. Who told the spies to see whether the land was good or bad, whether the people were strong or weak, and whether they lived in tents or strongholds? (Numbers 13:17–19)

18. Paul wrote that the wages of sin is what? (Romans 6:23)

19. Between Leah and Rachel, which sister was described as tender eyed? (Genesis 29:17)
20. How many days were the spies gone? (Numbers 13:25)
21. Who helped Levi kill a whole city of men to avenge their sister's honor? (Genesis 34:25)
22. The Bible records the sun, moon, and stars being commanded to do what for the Lord? (Psalm 148:3)

```
S  H  M  G  V  A  R  Y  T  S  I  M  E  L  I
T  A  V  A  I  L  S  A  T  F  Z  X  C  V  S
E  D  I  T  P  R  O  W  O  W  L  H  I  G  H
A  U  H  B  E  L  I  J  A  H  E  N  M  L  A
L  J  T  G  R  S  H  A  H  S  I  L  E  J  K
T  F  A  D  S  T  I  R  S  S  A  V  S  E
H  E  B  B  W  Q  A  A  F  O  R  E  V  E  R
E  R  B  A  R  N  N  O  R  N  E  V  E  S  T
S  H  A  M  G  A  R  E  A  P  E  N  B  O  Y
E  I  S  N  M  O  H  P  Y  T  O  U  D  M  Z
S  N  B  V  O  L  U  A  P  E  F  C  E  X  C
A  P  A  L  E  I  M  L  M  K  O  U  A  J  R
N  D  F  A  D  E  L  I  V  E  R  G  T  H  O
A  S  H  A  Q  W  S  T  A  T  T  I  H  S  W
M  R  E  B  A  B  Y  L  O  N  Y  E  L  L  O
```

Puzzle 45

1. What word means "one separated"? (Numbers 6:2)
2. When the Lord was leading the Israelites in the wilderness, He appeared as a pillar of what during the daytime? (Exodus 13:21)
3. What was Mishael's Babylonian name? (Daniel 1:7)
4. Whom did the people of Lystra insist that Barnabas was? (Acts 14:12 NIV)
5. What pieces of white clothing did they wear who were seen around the throne of heaven, serving God day and night in His temple? (Revelation 7:14-15)
6. How old were the Levites when they started their service in the temple? (2 Chronicles 31:17)
7. What type of animals devoured Jezebel after she was thrown from an upper window and died? (2 Kings 9:36)
8. To whom was God speaking when He said, "I am the Almighty God"? (Genesis 17:1)
9. At the marriage feast in Cana of Galilee, to whom did Jesus say, "Mine hour is not yet come"? (John 2:3-4)
10. What prophet did Jesus mention in connection with lepers? (Luke 4:27)
11. According to Ecclesiastes, there is a time to mourn and a time to do what? (Ecclesiastes 3:4)
12. Jesus said He did not come to destroy what but to fulfill it? (Matthew 5:17)
13. Who was known as "the Seer"? (2 Chronicles 9:29)
14. What does the name "Nabal" mean? (1 Samuel 25:25)
15. Herod made an oath to give up to how much of his kingdom to someone? (Mark 6:21, 23)
16. According to Matthew 16:26, Jesus asked this: For what is a man profited, if he shall gain the whole world, and yet lose what? (Matthew 16:26)

17. Who asked the question, "Who is my neighbor?" to Jesus? (Luke 10:25, 29)
18. Psalm 69:21 mentions what item that was offered to Jesus to drink on the cross? (Psalm 69:21)
19. Who was the first recorded Christian martyr? (Acts 7:54–60)
20. What's another word for "Preacher"? (Ecclesiastes 1:1)
21. To what did Naomi want to change her name? (Ruth 1:20)
22. Joshua said that for him and his house, he will do what to the Lord? (Joshua 24:2, 15)

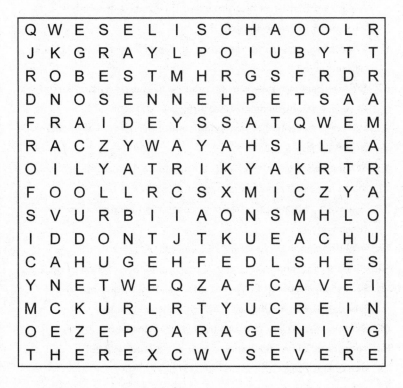

```
Q W E S E L I S C H A O O L R
J K G R A Y L P O I U B Y T T
R O B E S T M H R G S F R D R
D N O S E N N E H P E T S A A
F R A I D E Y S S A T Q W E M
R A C Z Y W A Y A H S I L E A
O I L Y A T R I K Y A K R T R
F O O L R C S X M I C Z Y A
S V U R B I I A O N S M H L O
I D D O N T J T K U E A C H U
C A H U G E H F E D L S H E S
Y N E T W E Q Z A F C A V E I
M C K U R L R T Y U C R E I N
O E Z E P O A R A G E N I V G
T H E R E X C W V S E V E R E
```

PUZZLE 46

1. Besides vinegar, what else couldn't a Nazarite drink? (Numbers 6:3)
2. What word means "the Lord watch between you and me"? (Genesis 31:49)
3. How many queens of Israel are mentioned by name? (1 Kings 16:31)
4. Who was the Persian ruler who allowed Nehemiah to rebuild Jerusalem? (Ezra 1:1)
5. Who shouldn't you visit frequently? (Proverbs 25:17)
6. Jesus said that He is the Alpha and the Omega, the beginning and what else? (Revelation 21:6)
7. Who threw dirt, stones, and dust on King David and cursed him? (2 Samuel 16:13)
8. Besides calming the water on the Sea of Galilee, what else did Jesus miraculously calm? (Matthew 8:26-27)
9. Which of the tribes of Israel had a mountain named after them? (1 Samuel 1:1)
10. What name means "the prince of devils"? (Matthew 12:24)
11. What was Hadassah's Persian name? (Esther 2:7)
12. Psalm 69:9 is a prophesy about Jesus doing what with the temple? (Psalm 69:9)
13. What name means "a stone"? (John 1:42)
14. Pharaoh decreed that all the baby Hebrew boys be killed because he was afraid that if Egypt went to war, those baby boys would have grown up, multiplied, and joined who? (Exodus 1:10)
15. What returned and covered the hosts of Pharaoh and there remained not so much as one of them? (Exodus 14:28)
16. What name was Gideon also known by? (Judges 7:1)
17. When John first saw the Lamb in heaven, what was the Lamb doing? (Revelation 5:6)
18. What did Peter enter that was empty? (John 20:6)
19. What major thing did Jesus do on a high mountain? (Matthew 17:1-2)

20. What New Testament writer said that we're not to swear by any oath but let our yea be yea and nay be nay? (James 5:12)

21. For the purposes of carrying the tabernacle and all its furnishings, the Levites were divided into how many groups? (Numbers 3:23–37)

22. What word means "weight"? (Daniel 5:27)

```
A  L  A  K  B  M  O  T  C  A  O  R  W  A  N
N  T  E  N  E  M  I  E  S  I  Z  E  S  D  H
J  Z  X  E  C  V  B  Z  S  H  I  M  E  I  X
S  E  M  A  J  G  H  J  P  K  L  R  M  N  G
B  F  A  R  E  B  E  A  R  A  U  D  S  C  N
E  S  T  H  R  E  E  E  W  G  H  Q  A  Y  I
E  A  C  H  U  R  N  E  I  G  H  B  O  R  D
L  H  H  U  B  Y  T  F  L  I  L  W  I  U  N
E  P  A  C  B  E  S  T  E  Z  T  I  O  S  A
Z  E  B  V  A  N  C  O  D  D  E  X  Z  P  T
E  C  L  E  A  N  S  I  N  G  K  B  N  M  S
B  N  H  R  L  J  K  E  I  E  E  O  U  L  A
E  S  T  H  E  R  N  G  W  F  L  O  D  B  Z
U  E  W  Q  M  I  A  R  H  P  E  K  A  S  M
B  N  Y  T  W  A  T  E  R  S  T  N  R  I  N
```

Puzzle 47

1. The ark of the covenant was carried by priests from which tribe? (Joshua 3:3)
2. What was "leaven of the Pharisees"? (Luke 12:1)
3. What was the name of the gate that the high priest Eliashib built during Nehemiah's time? (Nehemiah 3:1)
4. Who said, "Thou art the Christ"? (Matthew 16:16)
5. In one of Jesus' parables, what precious gem did the merchant find that prompted him to sell all he had in order to buy the gem? (Matthew 13:46)
6. Besides Elijah, which prophet did King Ahab hate? (1 Kings 22:8)
7. When the water turned to blood during the time of the ten plagues on Egypt, what happened to all the fish in the river? (Exodus 7:21)
8. Who did God ask, "Why are you angry?" (Genesis 4:6)
9. The first thing the Israelites built after returning to Jerusalem was what? (Ezra 3:3)
10. Who interceded for Paul when the believers at Jerusalem were reluctant to accept him as a convert? (Acts 9:27–28)
11. What moved the locusts into the Red Sea during the time of the ten plagues on Egypt? (Exodus 10:19)
12. What prophet told the king that the king would be as an ox and eat grass in the field? (Daniel 4:25)
13. In Jesus' illustration of how God wants to give us good things, the Lord said a father would not give his son a stone if he asked for what? (Luke 11:11)
14. Both Abraham and Isaac told the same half truth when they told foreign rulers that their wives were what relation to them? (Genesis 12:18–19; 26:9)
15. Who cried to the Lord in the wilderness when there was no water fit to drink? (Exodus 15:23–25)
16. Who was Samuel's mother? (1 Samuel 1:20)

17. What color garments would the church at Sardis wear if they overcame? (Revelation 3:5)

18. In the Old Testament, what priest was also a king? (Genesis 14:18)

19. How many books of prophecy are in the Old Testament? (Isaiah through Malachi)

20. Who had been in Rome for two years when the book of Acts ended? (Acts 28:30)

21. What was the surname of Jesus' disciples, James and John? (Matthew 4:21–22)

22. When the Israelites moved into the Promised Land, what found a permanent home in the city of Shiloh? (Joshua 18:1)

```
S S E V E N T E E N Q W S R B
A U H Y S T M T E N R A E A A
L R A E P I I O N P B L M T R
E H S J E H C K D A N I E L N
S O F D W P A G N S A Z L A A
M O A T E H I R I N G C C X B
W T O D A Y A Y E S T E H R U
I I B N V B H Y P O C R I S Y
N N N M Q R E S R A Z X Z S W
D A C D D A R R U P E T E R E
H V L B R E A D N C F R D T G
E I E U T D Y L U A P H E N B
A K V S T R A W B I C R K R Y
D E I D F R U I T N Z L P O L
A S L E E P Z E B E D E E D Z
```

PUZZLE 48

1. What river went dry as soon as the priests' feet touched the water's edge? (Joshua 3:15–16)

2. How many loaves of the Bread of Presence, or shewbread, were to be on the table in the tabernacle Sabbath after Sabbath? (Leviticus 24:5)

3. The group called "the sons of the prophets" was associated with what famous prophet? (2 Kings 6:1)

4. In Revelation 3:12, the church at Philadelphia was told that if they overcame, they would become pillars in what building of God? (Revelation 3:12)

5. What king claimed Ruth and Boaz as his great-grandparents? (Ruth 4:17)

6. Name the elderly priest whose wife bore a son who was a kinsman of Jesus? (Luke 1:13, 36)

7. What kind of tree supplied the wood for Aaron's rod that budded? (Numbers 17:8)

8. What prophet served as a prophet for four kings? (Isaiah 1:1)

9. What occupation did Bar-jesus, or Elymas, have when Paul struck him blind for his heresy? (Acts 13:6)

10. Who was Laban's brother-in-law? (Genesis 24:29)

11. Which Old Testament prophet mentioned both Daniel and Job? (Ezekiel 14:14)

12. The priest Urijah built an altar based on the design of an altar from what city? (2 Kings 16:11)

13. Who said, "Speak, for Your servant hears"? (1 Samuel 3:10)

14. For the Passover meal, what was to be without blemish or spot? (Exodus 12:5)

15. Which prophet said, "Can two walk together, except they be agreed?" (Amos 3:3)

16. How many of the plagues did Pharaoh's magicians duplicate? (Exodus 7:12, 22; 8:7)

17. Who did God ask, "What is that in your hand?" (Exodus 4:2)

18. In Jesus' parable of the Good Samaritan, what city was the man from Jerusalem who was robbed traveling to? (Luke 10:30)

19. How many sons did Gideon have? (Judges 8:30)

20. What king built the Lord's temple on Mount Moriah? (2 Chronicles 3:1)

21. What was the name of the gate that the sons of Hassenaah built? (Nehemiah 3:3)

22. What did Jesus put on the blind man's eyes before commanding him to wash in the pool of Siloam to be miraculously healed? (John 9:14–16)

```
I  D  M  T  U  M  A  J  O  R  D  A  N  I  T
T  Z  X  L  E  I  K  E  Z  E  B  C  V  E  Y
R  A  C  E  S  T  A  R  E  B  D  A  V  I  D
A  N  M  A  S  T  R  I  N  G  O  L  L  K  J
Z  L  I  F  S  O  R  C  E  R  E  R  U  O  S
C  A  L  I  K  E  L  H  H  W  G  F  D  S  A
H  C  C  S  I  R  L  O  T  S  A  M  U  E  L
E  E  Q  H  A  E  L  P  M  E  T  C  I  S  A
C  W  B  E  A  E  R  T  M  O  S  E  S  O  M
K  N  O  C  K  R  H  A  N  A  N  I  A  H  B
B  X  Y  A  C  H  I  T  M  A  I  Y  A  U  A
N  O  A  P  Z  T  X  A  C  V  B  N  C  M  I
D  A  L  M  O  N  D  L  S  E  V  E  N  T  Y
S  K  C  J  O  H  G  F  D  S  A  Q  W  E  R
D  N  C  A  H  S  I  L  E  S  Z  A  C  H  A
```

Puzzle 49

1. Who was Joshua the son of? (Exodus 33:11)
2. Who wrote the first song in the Bible and the last song in the Bible? (Exodus 15:1; Revelation 15:3)
3. How many sisters did the sons of Jacob have? (Genesis 34:1)
4. What tribe of Israel was famous for its left-handed sling users? (Judges 20:15-16)
5. What was the name of the servant Ahab commanded to go find Elijah? (1 Kings 18:3)
6. When Jesus stilled the storm, who were amazed and said that even the winds and the sea obey Him? (Matthew 8:27)
7. What priest's sons were called the "sons of Belial"? (1 Samuel 2:12)
8. Where was Abraham's servant, Eliezer, from? (Genesis 15:2)
9. The spies said the Promised Land flowed with what and honey? (Numbers 13:27)
10. Who lost all of his worldly possessions and his children in one day? (Job 1:13-19)
11. On what one day of the year could the high priest enter the Holy of Holies? (Leviticus 16:2, 33)
12. What tree is mentioned in Genesis and Revelation? (Genesis 2:9; Revelation 2:7)
13. To avenge himself over the loss of his wife, who burned the Philistine's crops? (Judges 15:3-5)
14. The Valley of Slaughter was originally known as the Valley of what? (Jeremiah 7:32)
15. Who did God promise to multiply his descendants as the stars in the heavens and as the sand on the seashore? (Genesis 22:17)
16. Fill in the blank: The Lord _____ the righteous. (Psalm 146:8)
17. Who used colors to describe sin? (Isaiah 1:18)
18. What was wrong with the vessel Jeremiah saw at the potter's shop? (Jeremiah 18:4)

19. Who wrote, "And when the Chief Shepherd shall appear, ye shall receive a crown of glory that fadeth not away"? (1 Peter 5:4)

20. Each of the living creatures that Ezekiel saw had how many faces? (Ezekiel 1:5–6)

21. After the tribes were split into the kingdoms of Israel and Judah, by what tribal name was the kingdom of Israel referred? (Isaiah 7:2)

22. What punishment was given to a man in the wilderness for picking up sticks on the Sabbath? (Numbers 15:32–36)

```
T H I S E L P I S C I D A W N
L Z L X C V T N E M E N O T A
O B A D I A H E E D W L T H U
V J K L M N B I M A S T I D T
E V E N I M A J N E B E E H I
S F D D U A L O L N I N E G C
T R E S S N I P X M O U N T M
I N R D U S I X A T Q M I L K
O R R E C C U E S I E A W A O
B O A Y S A V E U I S H U B N
L Z M I A R H P E M O A P O N
E L D X M O R J F O U R I U N
V I B S A M S O N S V B C A I
E F N M D L K B E E S A J T H
R E T E P R A Y E S E V E R E
```

Puzzle 50

1. Who quieted the people before Moses and challenged them to take the land immediately? (Numbers 13:30)

2. What type of blossoms were the holders on the tabernacle lampstands designed to look like? (Exodus 37:20)

3. What was the name of Herod's servant? (Luke 8:3)

4. Which tribe, because they were unable to occupy its allotted place in the Promised Land, took over somewhere else? (Judges 18:1)

5. Who was King Saul's father? (1 Samuel 9:1)

6. David and Jonathan used what objects as a signal between them? (1 Samuel 20:18–22)

7. Who circumcised Moses' son? (Exodus 4:25)

8. In Zechariah's vision, what object was seen flying? (Zechariah 5:1)

9. In whose vision of heaven did he see a sea of glass like crystal before the throne of heaven? (Revelation 4:6–7)

10. How did Egyptians view shepherds? (Genesis 46:34)

11. Who sang, "The horse and its rider He has thrown into the sea"? (Exodus 15:21)

12. What kind of tree did Deborah sit under? (Judges 4:5)

13. Fill in the blank: After His disciples plucked corn on the Sabbath, Jesus declared: "The Sabbath was made for man, and not man for the Sabbath: therefore the Son of man is _____ of the Sabbath." (Mark 2:23, 27–28)

14. Who appeared with Elijah and talked with Jesus on the Mount of Transfiguration? (Matthew 17:3)

15. On whose head was a garland of twelve stars? (Revelation 12:1)

16. Besides Jude, what other book in the Bible describes Michael fighting with Satan? (Revelation 12:7)

17. Samson killed one thousand Philistines with whose jawbone? (Judges 15:15 NIV)

18. What judge was the son of a harlot? (Judges 11:1)

19. Who said, "Through one man sin entered the world"? (Romans 5:12)

20. According to the Proverbs, a wise son makes his father glad but what type of son is the heaviness of his mother? (Proverbs 10:1)

21. Who helped Simeon kill a whole city of men to avenge their sister's honor? (Genesis 34:25)

22. How many pieces of gold were used to make the lampstand in the tabernacle? (Exodus 25:31)

I	N	T	D	N	E	T	E	R	P	R	O	D	O	T
P	Q	W	R	E	R	T	L	O	T	T	E	A	C	H
H	A	R	O	P	P	I	Z	E	R	O	F	N	Y	A
J	U	A	L	A	Y	J	U	G	V	J	O	H	N	V
E	C	D	E	L	I	V	E	S	T	I	O	X	N	E
P	P	A	L	M	O	N	D	P	T	I	L	O	N	E
T	O	I	L	Y	L	K	T	A	H	K	I	H	J	R
H	S	W	R	E	S	T	N	L	E	T	S	D	F	A
A	S	C	A	K	B	I	E	Z	A	C	H	S	I	K
H	M	N	R	N	M	B	S	L	V	H	C	A	X	E
P	A	U	L	O	Q	A	E	Z	X	U	S	R	H	E
O	D	E	B	D	L	V	S	N	O	Z	E	R	W	P
W	X	A	N	G	E	L	O	O	N	A	M	O	W	R
E	R	M	I	R	I	A	M	F	V	B	G	W	T	A
R	R	H	I	N	O	I	S	E	P	E	R	S	A	Y

Puzzle 51

1. Whoever calls upon the name of the Lord shall be what? (Romans 10:13)

2. Who described the believer's lively living hope this way: "To an inheritance, incorruptible, and undefiled, and that fadeth not away, reserved in heaven for you"? (1 Peter 1:34)

3. When Jesus prophesied that the temple would be destroyed, he described this as what would not be left one upon another? (Matthew 24:2)

4. Daniel purposed in his heart that he would not do what to himself? (Daniel 1:8)

5. Whose sin caused the defeat of Israel's army to Ai? (Joshua 7:1–4)

6. What was Jerusalem's original name? (Judges 19:10)

7. How many lepers looted the camp of the Syrians when God caused the Syrian army to flee? (2 Kings 7:3, 8)

8. Besides wine, what else couldn't a Nazarite drink? (Numbers 6:3)

9. Joseph made the Israelites swear an oath that after he died, they would take his bones out of what country? (Genesis 50:25)

10. Passover is also known as the Festival of what type of Bread? (Exodus 12:17)

11. Whom did the people of Lystra insist was Hermes because he was the chief speaker? (Acts 14:12)

12. What queen was thrown out of an upper window, died, and the dogs devoured her? (2 Kings 9:32–36)

13. What was Azariah's Babylonian name? (Daniel 1:7)

14. Which one of Jesus' twelve disciples was a Zealot? (Luke 6:15)

15. Who told the shepherds that the sign unto them would be a babe lying in a manger? (Luke 2:8–12)

16. Who was Ruth's sister-in-law? (Ruth 1:4)

17. According to Micah 6:8, we are to love mercy, walk humbly with God, and do what else? (Micah 6:8)

18. Mount Calvary is also known as what, which means "skull"? (Matthew 27:33)
19. Moses gained favor in Midian by getting what for the sisters? (Exodus 2:19–20)
20. Jesus' first recorded miracle was at Cana of Galilee when He turned water into what? (John 2:6–10)
21. What word means "a pause" or "the end"? (Psalm 3:8)
22. What was Israel's original name, before he wrestled with the angel? (Genesis 32:28)

```
D E F E R N L A G A M S A K N
P E Z X E C V J U B W I N E O
M K F N U S U B E J L M Y N M
A J O I N H F G T Z O O M S I
D T G O L G O T H A E D O F S
S A N D E E U D E H U B P O T
T A Y H A P R O S S H T E Y Y
I P A Y V D Q W E E P T T L A
L I D R E I T S E Y T Y E T R
L U N V N U N P G B E A R S N
I X A B E D N E G O E E Z U A
S S H P D C V B G C T N M J R
T L C A R S S E L A H C H O Y
E T A U T U M N W J R K J H X
N A M P A S T R A S L E G N A
```

Puzzle 52

1. According to Exodus 30:7-9, how often did the high priest burn incense on the golden altar?

2. How many altars did the tabernacle have? (Exodus 27:1-2)

3. Joshua 22:34 mentions an altar named Ed. According to the verse, what does Ed mean?

4. What was the altar made out of in Exodus 20:24?

5. What did Elijah use to make his altar on Mount Carmel? (1 Kings 18:31-32)

6. What part of the altar was to be grasped by someone seeking sanctuary? (1 Kings 2:28)

7. Where did Paul find an altar "to the Unknown God"? (Acts 17:22-23)

8. Who built seven altars three separate times? (Numbers 23: 1, 14, 29)

9. Who consecrated the altar of burnt offering in the tabernacle? (Exodus 29:44)

10. How many years was David king of Judah before he also became king of Israel? (2 Samuel 5:5)

11. Whom did Elijah anoint? (1 Kings 19:16)

12. How many times was David anointed to be king? (1 Samuel 16:3; 2 Samuel 2:4; 5:3)

13. Who anointed a pillar and made a vow to God at Bethel? (Genesis 31:13)

14. Who anointed Aaron and his sons to be priests? (Exodus 28:41)

15. Where, specifically, on his body was Aaron to be anointed? (Exodus 29:7)

16. What type of food in the tabernacle was anointed with oil? (Exodus 29:2)

17. Fill in the blank: The Lord called His feasts holy _____ . (Leviticus 23:2)

18. Fill in the blank: The Sabbath was to be a day of _____ . (Leviticus 23:3)

19. The fourteenth day of the first month was what? (Leviticus 23:5)

20. Fill in the blank: During the Feast of Firstfruits, the priest was to wave a _____ before the Lord. (Leviticus 23:10–11)

```
Y  A  D  Y  R  E  V  E  S  R  E  F  A  W  P
B  T  R  E  X  T  S  E  R  A  G  N  S  K  A
A  H  O  W  X  Q  U  H  I  F  O  N  E  R  E
S  E  V  E  N  B  C  V  A  B  O  S  I  N  P
Z  N  A  D  V  I  M  E  F  I  E  D  L  W  A
E  S  T  W  Y  E  H  Q  T  N  E  D  C  H  S
K  M  O  S  E  S  U  A  O  G  A  I  S  K  S
S  W  L  O  U  F  C  T  R  E  G  I  K  M  O
N  P  X  D  U  O  S  O  H  T  L  B  S  U  V
R  B  O  W  V  E  O  S  J  E  S  I  S  Z  E
O  G  A  N  V  M  I  P  O  Y  A  R  E  Q  R
H  X  O  L  S  H  A  R  T  Y  F  R  N  H  V
E  C  E  J  A  C  O  B  B  W  A  E  T  P  L
H  W  V  E  Q  A  Y  B  N  M  I  O  I  H  T
T  H  R  E  E  W  M  Y  E  K  G  O  W  T  A
```

Puzzle 53

1. According to 2 Samuel 14:20, which of the following is an attribute of the angel of the Lord?

2. How many times did the angel of the Lord speak to Abraham during the attempted sacrifice of Isaac? (Genesis 22:10–18)

3. What animal saw the angel of the Lord? (Numbers 22:23)

4. In Isaiah 63:9, Isaiah calls the angel of the Lord "the Angel of His _____."

5. Who was called the "son of the morning"? (Isaiah 14:12)

6. How many types of angels are mentioned in the Bible? (Genesis 3:24; Isaiah 6:2; Jude 9)

7. What type of angel was on top of the ark of the covenant? (Exodus 25:18)

8. What angel was associated with Passover? (Exodus 12:23)

9. What angel is described in the book of Daniel as "one of the chief princes"? (Daniel 10:13)

10. Who can appear as an angel of light? (2 Corinthians 11:14)

11. What prophet referred to the cherubim as "living creatures"? (Ezekiel 10:20)

12. How many wings do cherubim have? (Ezekiel 1:6)

13. How many wings do seraphim have? (Isaiah 6:2)

14. What did the angels do when God created the world? (Job 38:7 NIV)

15. How many angels appeared to the women who came to Jesus' tomb? (Luke 24:4)

16. How many angels first appeared to the shepherds to announce Jesus' birth? (Luke 2:9, 13)

17. To whom was Jesus speaking when He said that children have angels? (Matthew 18:10)

18. What do the angels in heaven say? (Revelation 5:11–12)

19. What does Psalm 78:24–25 refer to as angels' food?

20. What devout Gentile saw an angel? (Acts 10:3)

```
E  S  D  S  E  L  P  I  C  S  I  D  S  I  H
W  O  R  T  H  Y  I  S  T  H  E  L  A  M  B
Y  E  K  N  O  D  W  S  K  O  L  P  Y  L  C
I  K  K  B  S  H  R  A  F  T  W  O  T  E  D
K  E  E  R  H  T  Z  U  Q  R  J  V  Y  I  I
E  M  Y  C  A  M  I  B  U  R  E  H  C  K  F
C  I  H  T  A  D  O  M  O  N  E  X  Y  E  O
N  C  B  L  U  C  I  F  E  R  I  K  L  Z  U
E  H  A  T  H  E  D  E  S  T  R  O  Y  E  R
S  A  G  H  P  E  S  U  I  L  E  N  R  O  C
E  E  N  A  T  A  S  H  A  Z  U  Q  N  M  T
R  L  P  U  L  H  S  N  E  X  E  S  H  W  A
P  H  O  W  X  C  N  Q  U  I  V  B  I  X  R
D  H  U  K  X  A  G  S  E  D  R  C  Y  X  I
S  Y  E  A  M  O  D  S  I  W  E  G  H  P  S
```

Puzzle 54

1. How many of each clean animal did Noah take on the ark? (Genesis 7:2)

2. Which of the following is an unclean animal? Cattle, sheep, grasshoppers, camels. (Leviticus 11:4)

3. Which is longer: the list of clean animals or unclean animals? (Leviticus 11:1–47)

4. Is the following a description of a clean or an unclean animal? ". . .every flying insect that creeps on all fours, which have jointed legs upon their feet." (Leviticus 11:21)

5. What kind of animals helped Samson burn the grain fields of his enemies? Lightning bugs, lions, donkey, foxes. (Judges 15:3–5)

6. What kind of bird, released from the ark, brought an olive leaf back to Noah? (Genesis 8:11)

7. What do these three things have in common? Arcturus, Orion, Pleiades. (Job 9:9)

8. What animals were the Israelites not to muzzle as it was treading grain (NIV) or corn (KJV)? (Deuteronomy 25:4)

9. After Adam and Eve sinned, God provided clothing for them made of _____ _____. (Genesis 3:21)

10. What animal did God provide as a substitute burnt offering as Abraham prepared to offer Isaac? (Genesis 22:13)

11. When it saw the angel of the Lord, a donkey spoke to whom? (Numbers 22:27–28 NIV)

12. The psalmist said he longed for God even as a _____ panted for streams of water. (Psalm 42:1 NIV)

13. What animal did Jesus ride for His triumphal entry into Jerusalem? (John 12:14–15 NIV)

14. What animal did Goliath compare himself to when he saw David approaching him? (1 Samuel 17:43)

15. Peter likened Christ's atonement to a " _____ without _____ and without spot." (1 Peter 1:19)

16. What creature of the wilderness does Malachi describe as laying waste to Esau's heritage? (Malachi 1:3)

17. What colors are the four horses mentioned in Revelation 6? (Revelation 6:2–8)

18. What is the strongest of beasts, according to Proverbs? (Proverbs 30:30)

19. How many disciples did Jesus ask to retrieve Him a donkey? (Matthew 21:1–2 NIV)

20. When some young people mocked Elisha by calling him "bald head," what animals did God send to punish them? (2 Kings 2:23–24)

```
W E F R G N A C S R A E B Z O
X M L S N O G A R D N M Y E T
Q A F K E I P O C E T I H W N
Z A I U T L R G H X E L A M B
U L H I L P Y E K N O D W E N
W A T B S N I K S L A M I N A
Y B V E W R T G S Y M E E F H
R C O N S T E L L A T I O N S
H D X E K I D E R O K L S N I
C O E V C M N O P A L E K A M
X L N N A E L C N M X U T E E
L K Z A L T E E V O D I W L L
Y E R X B A M B F J K E O C B
A Y E S R I A P N E V E S N G
R G O D W E C R G A T P L U A
```

PUZZLE 55

1. Which of the following was not an apostle? Paul, Peter, Matthias, John Mark. (Romans 1:1; Matthew 10:2; Acts 1:26)

2. Which book of the Bible is specifically named for the apostles? (Acts, book overview)

3. Who was the first apostle sent to a Gentile? (Acts 10:19-22)

4. The apostle who spoke to the Ethiopian eunuch was. . .Philip, Peter, Stephen, or Paul? (Acts 8:26-35)

5. Who brought Paul to the apostles? (Acts 9:27)

6. How did Paul become an apostle? (1 Corinthians 1:1)

7. Paul said he was the chief of sinners (1 Timothy 1:15) and the _____ of the apostles. (1 Corinthians 15:9)

8. What covered the poles used to carry the ark of the covenant? (Exodus 25:13)

9. Fill in the blank: "At that time the LORD set apart the tribe of _____ to carry the ark of the covenant of the LORD." (Deuteronomy 10:8 NIV)

10. What happened to Eli when he learned his two sons had been killed and the ark captured by the enemy? (1 Samuel 4:18)

11. Who built a temple for the ark? (1 Kings 8:12, 17-21)

12. When in the tabernacle, the ark was in an area called what? (Hebrews 9:2-4 NIV)

13. On what mountain was the ark of the covenant built? (Exodus 24:15-25:22)

14. What did the Philistines return with the ark of the covenant when they returned it to Israel? (1 Samuel 6:4, 11)

15. Where will the ark of the covenant ultimately be found? (Revelation 11:19)

16. Who was the last person on earth to see the ark of the covenant? (Revelation 11:19)

17. What prophet sat on a hill while God sent fire to burn up the army sent to capture him? (2 Kings 1:9-10)

18. How many armies did God send fire on? (2 Kings 1:11–12)

19. Fill in the blank: The army that fought with pitchers and lamps shouted, "The sword of the LORD and of _____ ." (Judges 7:18)

20. Who had to build a wall with one hand while holding his sword in the other? (Nehemiah 4:17–18)

```
A  D  U  S  H  I  J  A  P  E  W  A  Q  M  X
P  I  L  I  H  P  M  I  H  G  I  D  E  O  N
H  E  X  N  J  O  C  K  L  O  P  Z  E  S  S
N  D  N  A  U  Q  W  E  I  M  N  A  V  T  D
O  X  Y  I  F  H  S  T  N  E  V  A  E  H  O
J  Y  T  E  N  I  X  S  A  F  R  E  C  O  R
W  E  R  Y  T  B  V  A  N  W  A  J  K  L  E
C  A  H  A  J  I  L  E  J  U  C  I  V  Y  M
H  K  W  A  R  C  A  L  L  E  D  M  O  P  E
D  I  H  A  I  M  E  H  E  N  S  D  U  L  N
A  B  A  R  N  A  B  A  S  X  Y  R  P  A  E
B  U  T  E  A  H  P  E  T  E  R  O  D  C  D
Y  N  O  M  O  L  O  S  C  Q  U  G  L  E  L
A  L  T  R  E  X  K  R  A  M  N  H  O  J  O
M  E  I  E  C  I  M  N  E  D  L  O  G  A  G
```

PUZZLE 56

1. From what location did Jesus teach about the Beatitudes? (Matthew 5:1)

2. Fill in the blanks: Blessed are the _____ _____ _____ : for theirs in the kingdom of heaven. (Matthew 5:3)

3. Fill in the blanks: Blessed are they that _____ : for they shall be _____ . (Matthew 5:4)

4. Fill in the blank: Blessed are the _____ : for they shall inherit the earth. (Matthew 5:5)

5. Fill in the blanks: Blessed are they which do _____ and _____ after righteousness: for they shall be _____ . (Matthew 5:6)

6. Fill in the blanks: Blessed are the _____ : for they shall obtain _____ . (Matthew 5:7)

7. Fill in the blanks: Blessed are the _____ _____ _____ : for they shall see God. (Matthew 5:8)

8. Fill in the blank: Blessed are the _____ : for they shall be called the children of God. (Matthew 5:9)

9. Fill in the blank: Blessed are they which are persecuted for _____ sake: for theirs is the kingdom of heaven. (Matthew 5:10)

10. Fill in the blanks: Blessed are ye, when men shall _____ you, and _____ you, and shall say all manner of evil against you _____ , for my sake. (Matthew 5:11)

11. Fill in the blanks: Rejoice, and be exceedingly glad: for _____ is your _____ in heaven. (Matthew 5:12)

E T U C E S R E P E L T Y A S
R A U H G K D R A W E R S H S
L Y O S R E K A M E C A E P E
A L J G E A R E L I V E R O N
X E B U A L I M K Y E H S A S
U S I H T A Z F C O I N W T U
A L F P J D E R A B N I S U O
L A I E D Q E T Y L K E N M E
U F L S U M I T A T S R I H T
F O L I G D A K R E L U A S H
I K E E M O A W L O V P T E G
C I D W O L I O V N F U N X I
R E G N U H F S W U I M U P R
E Z T I R I P S N I R O O P E
M U Q S N E W M N B E L M C A

Puzzle 57

1. What two books of the Bible do not mention God by name?
2. What two books have the census of all who returned from Babylon? (Ezra 2; Nehemiah 7)
3. What book of the Bible contains the Golden Rule? (Matthew 7:12)
4. What book of the Bible mentions the stars singing? (Job 38:7)
5. What book of the Bible is named for a tribe of Israel? (Leviticus, book overview)
6. How many chapters does the book of Daniel have?
7. What book of the Bible has more references to angels than any other book of the Bible?
8. In which two books of the Bible do we read of Michael having a face-to-face confrontation with Satan? (Jude 9; Revelation 12:7)
9. Which book of the Bible contains the story of David and Goliath? (1 Samuel 17)
10. How many books of the Bible have only one chapter? (Obadiah, Philemon, 2 John, 3 John, Jude)
11. What book of the New Testament is totally dedicated to describing God's love for us?
12. What is the longest book in the Bible?
13. What subject does the longest chapter in the Bible deal with? (Psalm 119:1)
14. How many books are in the Old Testament?
15. How many books are in the New Testament?
16. What is the last book of the Old Testament?
17. The first five books of the Bible are commonly referred to as the books of _____ .
18. Fill in the blank: The book of Revelation is the revelation of _____ . (Revelation 1:1)

```
A G H E D R I H T Y T N E W T
N O I T A L E V E R J U D E G
Z D A R Z E E D C V O K M N O
A S D T R U U O I P B X Z O N
U L T Q E M V W E H T T A M E
G A S N F A R T X F Z V A O V
H W I O E S U C I T I V E L E
I L R I D T W L Y A E V L O S
H E H T Q S M L A S P U E S Y
C V C A Y R H Q E W F N B F T
A L S L F I R S T J O H N O N
L E U E R F T H U F R T Y G E
A W S V H A I M E H E N M N W
M T E E N I N Y T R I H T O T
D A J R H Y R E V R E H T S E
```

Puzzle 58

1. What portion of Adam's anatomy did God remove to create a companion for the man? (Genesis 2:22)

2. Where did Peter find a coin to pay the temple tax? (Matthew 17:27)

3. What personal item did Ruth's kinsman present to Boaz as an indication he would not redeem Ruth? (Ruth 4:6–7)

4. Who led a dance of joy wearing only a linen cloth when the ark of the covenant arrived in Jerusalem? (2 Samuel 6:14–15)

5. When Jesus healed the Gadarene demoniac, where did the demons go? (Luke 8:33)

6. What king of Israel solved a child custody dispute by proposing that the child be cut in half? (1 Kings 3:3, 25–27)

7. What prophet was taken alive to heaven in a whirlwind? (2 Kings 2:11)

8. What young prince was hidden in the temple by his aunt for six years to avoid the wrath of Queen Athaliah? (2 Kings 11:2–3)

9. Who went to sleep while Paul was preaching and fell from a window to his death, but was revived by the apostle? (Acts 20:9–12)

10. What did Jesus say He would arrive in when He returns to earth "with power and great glory"? (Luke 21:27)

11. How many men ended up in Gideon's army? (Judges 7:6–7)

12. How many swords did the disciples take with them when they followed Jesus to the Garden of Gethsemane? (Luke 22:38)

13. What rank did Naaman hold in the army of Syria? (2 Kings 5:1 NIV)

14. According to Revelation 19:14, what are the armies in heaven clothed in?

15. How long did the Philistines keep the ark of the covenant? (1 Samuel 6:1)

16. The first blessing of the Bible was pronounced upon sea creatures and _____ . (Genesis 1:21–22)

17. How many angels went to save Lot from the destruction of his city? (Genesis 19:1)

18. Jesus said it was easier for a _____ to go through the eye of a needle than for a rich man to enter heaven. (Matthew 19:24)

19. What military rank did Cornelius, a Gentile convert to Christianity, hold? (Acts 10:1)

20. Who said, "Behold, I tell you a mystery"? (1 Corinthians 15:51)

A	S	L	J	F	S	E	V	L	U	A	P	K	D	A
B	I	S	A	S	D	E	K	G	F	S	I	U	O	P
A	R	Y	E	T	I	P	L	J	F	E	V	E	S	N
G	D	O	U	X	W	N	E	N	I	L	E	N	I	F
C	E	C	T	H	T	O	Y	N	O	M	O	L	O	S
N	R	O	Y	D	Y	V	L	K	D	E	O	H	S	U
O	D	M	C	H	E	H	S	A	O	J	X	T	F	K
I	N	M	H	S	G	Z	V	I	P	O	L	U	N	M
R	U	A	U	E	N	I	W	S	T	D	U	O	L	C
U	H	N	S	L	D	E	Q	U	W	I	T	M	J	A
T	E	D	Z	I	Y	R	L	B	O	E	A	H	L	M
N	E	E	D	J	B	I	R	D	S	Y	R	S	H	E
E	R	R	D	A	E	V	E	J	H	N	M	I	O	L
C	H	U	F	H	A	I	P	B	N	E	V	F	B	A
O	T	S	I	S	H	T	N	O	M	N	E	V	E	S

Puzzle 59

After reading the following statements, answer a simple question: Who?

1. A choice young man, and a goodly: and there was not among the children of Israel a goodlier person than he: from his shoulders and upward he was higher than any of the people. (1 Samuel 9:2)

2. He will be a wild man; his hand will be against every man, and every man's hand against him; and he shall dwell in the presence of all his brethren. (Genesis 16:11-12)

3. This he said, not that he cared for the poor; but because he was a thief, and had the bag, and bare what was put therein. (John 12:4-6)

4. Now he was ruddy, and withal of a beautiful countenance, and goodly to look to. (1 Samuel 16:12-13)

5. Fill in the blank: Among them that are born of women there hath not risen a greater than ____ ____ ____ : not withstanding he that is least in the kingdom of heaven is greater than he. (Matthew 11:11)

6. And, behold, there was a man. . .which was the chief among the publicans, and he was rich. And he sought to see Jesus who he was; and could not for the press, because he was little of stature. (Luke 19:2-3)

7. [He] did evil in the sight of the LORD above all that were before him . . . .[He] did more to provoke the LORD God of Israel to anger than all the kings of Israel that were before him. (1 Kings 16:30, 33)

8. Full of faith and power, he did great wonders and miracles among the people. . . . And all that sat in the council, looking stedfastly on him, saw his face as it had been the face of an angel. (Acts 6:8, 15)

9. To bring. . .the queen before the king with the crown royal, to shew the people and the princes her beauty: for she was fair to look on. (Esther 1:11)

10. And when Jehu was come to Jezreel. . .she painted her face, and tired her head, and looked out at a window. (2 Kings 9:30)

11. [He] wist not that the skin of his face shone while he talked with him. (Exodus 34:29)

12. Howbeit the hair of his head began to grow again after he was shaven. (Judges 16:22)

13. And at the end of ten days whose four countenances appeared fairer and fatter in flesh than all the children which did eat the portion of the king's meat. (Daniel 1:11-15)

14. He hardened his heart, and hearkened not unto them; as the LORD had said. (Exodus 8:15)

15. She dwelt under the palm tree. . .between Ramah and Bethel in mount Ephraim: and the children of Israel came up to her for judgment. (Judges 4:4-5)

16. Because the preacher was wise, he still taught the people knowledge; yea, he gave good heed, and sought out, and set in order many proverbs. (Ecclesiastes 1:1; 12:9)

17. Fill in the blank: Let us hear the conclusion of the whole matter: Fear God, and keep his commandments: for this is the whole duty of _____ . (Ecclesiastes 12:13)

18. Her husband, being a just man, and not willing to make her a public example, was minded to put her away privily. (Matthew 1:19)

19. Woe is me! for I am undone; because I am a man of unclean lips, and I dwell in the midst of a people of unclean lips: for mine eyes have seen the King, the LORD of hosts. (Isaiah 6:5)

20. Fill in the blank: But in all Israel there was none to be so much praised as_____for his beauty: from the sole of his foot even to the crown of his head there was no blemish in him. And when he polled his head, (for it was at every year's end that he polled it: because the hair was heavy on him, therefore he polled it:) he weighed the hair of his head at two hundred shekels after the king's weight. (2 Samuel 14:25–26)

A	B	S	O	P	N	L	E	A	H	S	I	M	K	U
E	L	J	S	E	F	T	L	E	A	M	H	S	I	Q
N	E	H	P	E	T	S	K	Q	U	O	L	T	N	A
A	B	O	B	V	B	I	A	E	E	S	D	O	G	B
P	E	A	L	A	M	T	U	M	O	E	X	I	S	S
C	Z	R	M	S	H	P	N	A	S	S	Z	R	A	A
H	E	A	O	H	H	A	O	M	V	O	W	A	U	H
I	J	H	L	T	A	B	M	A	V	O	N	C	L	A
M	H	P	A	I	I	E	O	D	B	N	Y	S	E	I
H	A	X	S	E	R	H	L	X	I	M	P	I	I	N
A	R	N	B	Z	A	T	O	C	H	V	R	S	N	A
I	O	B	A	U	Z	N	S	I	Y	T	A	A	A	N
A	B	S	U	E	A	H	C	C	A	Z	O	D	D	A
S	E	L	O	P	R	O	E	H	T	Y	C	U	S	H
I	D	N	M	W	E	J	H	P	E	S	O	J	Q	U

Puzzle 60

1. Fill in the blank: We shall not all sleep, but we shall all be _____ . (1 Corinthians 15:51)

2. Fill in the blanks: In a _____ , in the _____ of an eye, at the last trumpet. (1 Corinthians 15:52)

3. Fill in the blank: Husbands are to love their wives like Christ loved the _____ . (Ephesians 5:25)

4. The last mystery mentioned in the Bible concerns Jesus, the apostle John, the antichrist, or Babylon? (Revelation 17:5, 7)

5. According to Psalm 90:10, how many are the days of our years?

6. How many spies sent into the Promised Land gave an unfavorable report? (Numbers 13)

7. How many were in Jacob's family (including Joseph's family) when Jacob moved to Egypt? (Exodus 1:5)

8. The boy's lunch that Jesus used to feed the five thousand consisted of what? (Matthew 14:17)

9. If someone was too poor to afford a lamb for a sacrifice for the birth of their child, how many turtledoves could be substituted? (Leviticus 12:8)

10. How many mites did the widow give? (Mark 12:42)

11. How many precious stones decorated the front of the high priest's breastplate? (Exodus 28:21)

12. How many men composed Gideon's initial army? (Judges 7:3)

13. How many days did Noah wait after sending out the raven and the dove before he sent out the dove again? (Genesis 8:10)

14. What famous king had seven hundred wives? (1 Kings 11:3)

15. How many cubits did Jesus say we can add to our stature? (Matthew 6:27)

16. Approximately how many souls were added to the church on the day of Pentecost? _____ thousand. (Acts 2:41)

17. How many days did Daniel and his friends eat "pulse and water"? (Daniel 1:12)

18. How old was Jesus when Mary and Joseph found Him in the temple? (Luke 2:42-43)

19. How many people did God tell Elijah there were who had never bowed the knee to Baal? _____ thousand. (1 Kings 19:18)

20. How many men did Jesus send out to arrive in cities before He did? (Luke 10:1)

```
E R T A E N M D N A S U O H T
D W H Q N T Y H J O I B N S W
M L R P O Y Y T N E V E S E O
X N E Q N O M O L O S N B F D
C N E G K E V L E W T I R Y U
J O L T Y W X M Y T N E V E S
O X R W H J K L Y E N M A R Y
W T S E V E N I N T N E M O M
T W P L U T A D E G N A H C V
Y O U V X I H P V H N B H S L
T F X E N E R B E H C U R E X
R I X M B L I U S M K R T E H
I S E V A O L E V I F N U R V
H H Y B A B Y L O N T R E H J
T A N E T G N I L K N I W T C
```

PUZZLE 61

1. How many years was the ark of the covenant kept in Kirjath-jearim? (1 Samuel 7:2)

2. How many days and nights was Jonah in the belly of the great fish? (Jonah 1:17)

3. One hundred and _____ - _____ fish were caught in the net when Jesus told His disciples to cast the net on the right side of the boat. (John 21:6, 11)

4. How many days did the spies Moses sent search in the Promised Land? (Numbers 13:25)

5. Who was a songwriter, shepherd, and harpist? (2 Samuel 22:1; 1 Samuel 17:14-15; 1 Samuel 16:23)

6. Who was spokesperson to Pharaoh, idol maker, priest? (Exodus 5:1; 32:3-4; 29:5)

7. Who was tender of the garden, namer of animals, father of all mankind? (Genesis 2:15, 20)

8. Who was slave messenger, beloved brother? (Philemon 12, 16 NKJV)

9. Who was ruler, Pharisee, defender of Jesus? (John 3:1, 7:50-51)

10. The Lord chose them to stand in His presence, to serve Him, to be His ministers. (2 Chronicles 29:4, 11)

11. Everyone in distress, everyone in debt, everyone discontent, about four hundred in number. (1 Samuel 22:1-2)

12. Who was filled with the Spirit of God and wisdom in understanding, skilled in all manner of workmanship, and designed artistic works? (Exodus 31:2-4 NKJV)

13. Works with her hands, provides food for her household, plants a vineyard, helps the poor and needy, makes tapestry. (Proverbs 31:10, 13-22)

14. Who was priest, father of bad sons, raised Samuel? (1 Samuel 2:11-12, 18)

15. Whatever he did, the Lord made it prosper. (Genesis 39:23 NKJV)

16. What two types of birds did Noah send out from the ark to see if the waters were receding? (Genesis 8:6–8)

17. What type of bird brought food to Elijah? (1 Kings 17:4)

18. Fill in the blank: They that wait upon the LORD shall renew their strength; they shall mount up with wings as _____ . (Isaiah 40:31)

19. Fill in the blank: In Song of Solomon 2:11–12, the winter is past and the voice of the _____ is heard. (Song of Solomon 2:11–12)

20. What type of bird did Jesus say that not one falls to the ground without God knowing about it? (Matthew 10:29)

```
O V E S E V O D E L T R U T N
C I Y T S A M N E O P L E K J
T R A V E N O L U I X V E W A
N T I S U M I S E N O V C N M
M U B E Z A L E L D W E R T U
S O N T P I U E F Y D R A M S
W U E I X S W Q I Y T I U A U
O S M V L E K E F A B R V D M
R W S E M L X H T A R T O A E
R O D L I G O P Y R T Y U F D
A M I D W A B E T T N L K E O
P A V L P E U S H A N T R E C
S N A A S D N O R A A E X R I
O P D I U R T J E S H G W H N
Z A F G H R A V E N S W E T Z
```

PUZZLE 62

1. Fill in the blanks: when Satan spoke to God about Job, he said that God had blessed the _____ of Job's _____ . (Job 1:10)

2. The blessing of the Lord, it maketh, rich, wise, courage, or love? (Proverbs 10:22)

3. Fill in the blanks: It is more blessed to _____ than to _____ . (Acts 20:35)

4. Fill in the blank: James said, "Out of the same _____ proceed blessing and cursing." (James 3:10)

5. Fill in the blank: Jesus said, "As long as I am in the world, I am the _____ of the world." (John 9:5)

6. To what group of people did the neighbors take the man after they saw he was healed? (John 9:13)

7. Fill in the blank: The man told Jesus: "Lord, I _____ . And he worshipped him." (John 9:38)

8. Who said that he was eyes to the blind, feet to the lame, a father to the poor? Abraham, Isaiah, Job, or Paul? (Job 29:15–16)

9. What prophet asked God to strike the Syrians blind? (2 Kings 6:18–20)

10. Whom did Jesus send to restore Saul's (Paul's) sight? (Acts 9:17–18)

11. What sorcerer did Paul strike blind in the name of the Lord? (Acts 13:6–11)

12. Of whom did Jesus say that they were the blind leaders of the blind? (Matthew 15:12–14)

13. Which of the seven churches in Revelation did Jesus say was blind? (Revelation 3:14, 17)

14. God said that He had blinded His people's eyes and hardened their hearts lest they should understand and be _____ . (John 12:40)

15. What blinds the eyes of the wise and twists the words of the righteous? (Deuteronomy 16:19 NIV)

16. Which of the following did NOT see a host of angels? Jacob, Peter, shepherds at Bethlehem, or John? (Genesis 28:10–12; Luke 2:8–14; Revelation 7:11)

17. How many angels went to save Lot from the destruction of his city? (Genesis 19:1)

18. Jesus said it was easier for a _____ to go through the eye of a needle than for a rich man to enter heaven. (Matthew 19:24)

19. What military rank did Cornelius, a Gentile convert to Christianity, hold? (Acts 10:1–2)

20. Fill in the blank: But _____ found grace in the eyes of the Lord. (Genesis 6:8)

```
S H A O N E R T H J K L O B X
Y R Y X A E C I D O A L P W E
A S E E S I R A H P E T E R T
H G A R E M N V X Z S G H U Q
K L Q M U I O D E L A E H F Y
E R T V Y R E B I R B T O J N
T E V N M L U T M B U L L K O
P H A R I S E E S O R T I K I
O K J H G F K L M S E S G U R
L I A R E D H T Y D C I H V U
E F H X B V C N M N E A T U T
M A S Q U K I G H A I N B M N
A L I K Y T R G J H V A R F E
C O L R T Y C O W R E N D I C
E V E I L E B A W J K A T Y H
```

Puzzle 63

1. What two pairs of brothers were Jesus' disciples? _____ and _____ , _____ and _____ . (Matthew 4:18–21)

2. Which one of his brothers did Absalom kill to avenge his sister, Tamar's, honor? (2 Samuel 13:28–29)

3. Which brother of Solomon tried to take Solomon's throne and then claimed sanctuary in the temple? (1 Kings 1:50)

4. How many brothers did Abram have? (Genesis 11:27)

5. Fill in the blank: Proverbs 17:17 says that a brother is born for _____ .

6. David was the youngest of how many brothers? (1 Samuel 16:10–11)

7. A brother offended is harder to win than what? (Proverbs 18:19)

8. Who was born grasping his brother's heel? (Genesis 25:26)

9. Fill in the blank: 1 John 2:10 says that he who loves his brother abides in the _____ .

10. Of which two brothers was it said that one was hairy and one was smooth skinned? (Genesis 27:11 NKJV)

11. On the first trip, how many of Joseph's brothers came to Egypt? (Genesis 42:3–4)

12. Fill in the blank: Joseph told his brothers, "It was not you who sent me here, but _____ ." (Genesis 45:8)

13. On the second trip for grain, who else came with the brothers? (Genesis 43:8–15)

14. Which kingdom of Israel did Assyria take captive: northern or southern? (1 Chronicles 5:26)

15. Who was king when Assyria took Israel captive? (2 Kings 17:6)

16. Who was king of Assyria at this time? (2 Kings 17:3)

17. What nation did the king of Israel try to get to help him fight Assyria? (2 Kings 17:4)

18. Which kingdom of Israel did Babylon take captive: northern or southern? (2 Chronicles 36:15—17 NIV)

19. Who was king of Israel at this time? (2 Kings 24:1)

20. Fill in the blank: Israel became a captive of Egypt because "there arose up a new king over Egypt, which knew not _____." (Exodus 1:8)

```
T H R U I L M I K A I O H E J
B E V Q H D N I M A J N E B A
O H N G O U B V K L E I G H T
C I R E S E N A M L A H S A H
A H T P H G A U N B O C A J G
J P I Z E Y W A X N E G V I I
D E N M A P T Y W U O N B N L
N S X C M T N U I D Y N F O X
A O S O U T H E R N Y T M D N
U J Y W E N Y U E X R W V A H
A S T R O N G C I T Y E T K O
S Y T I S R E V D A Y A T E J
E O V C Q U I N T M J A M E S
D E R T Y U I G W E R D N A P
Y G N R E H T R O N G R T E A
```

Puzzle 64

1. Fill in the blanks: Pharaoh commanded that every son who was born should be cast into the _____ , but every daughter could be _____ _____ . (Exodus 1:22 NKJV)

2. The Egyptians were in _____ of the Israelites. (Exodus 1:12 NKJV)

3. How old was the youngest king of Judah when he began to reign? (2 Kings 11:1–4, 21)

4. How old was the second youngest king of Judah when he began to reign? (2 Kings 22:1)

5. How old was Jarius's daughter when Jesus raised her from the dead? (Luke 8:42)

6. Psalm 127:3 says that children are a _____ from the Lord.

7. Who said, "For this child I prayed"? (1 Samuel 1:27)

8. What child, when he was called in the night, said, "Speak; for thy servant heareth"? (1 Samuel 3:10)

9. In which book of the Bible is the following verse found: "Children, obey your parents in the Lord: for this is right?" (Ephesians 6:1)

10. Isaiah 11:6 says, "A little child shall lead them." What will the child lead?

11. What ruler killed all the male children two years old and younger in Bethlehem and its surrounding districts? (Matthew 2:16–18)

12. In what church were the disciples first called Christians? (Acts 11:26)

13. What church was Lydia a part of? (Acts 16:14)

14. When certain people told the church in Jerusalem that everyone had to be circumcised to be saved, who rebuked them? (Acts 15:7)

15. Who were the leaders at the church of Corinth whom Paul stayed with? (Acts 18:1–2)

16. What did the apostles appoint in every church? (Acts 14:23)
17. Which church sent Paul and Barnabas on their first missionary journey? (Acts 13:1-3)
18. Which church was told it was lukewarm? (Revelation 3:14, 16)
19. Which church was told they had a Jezebel among them? (Revelation 2:18, 20)
20. Which church was told they dwell where Satan's throne is? (Revelation 2:12-13)

```
D A E G H S E G A T I R E H A
X A L I V E S A M U E L I A R
Z N E W E V R P A F G H J N I
A T P R P E T R E N G H E N T
S I H E D N N I L V T K J A A
O O E C T V B S A E L I R H Y
M C S S X E O C R L P E O J H
A H I R D W R I I H M U W C T
G X A E S A F L T K R H D T H
R A N D R T Y L A L R E E H U
E Z S L Q O I A Y V B R V G T
P V E E Y T W J H K L O A I Z
L A O D I C E A T E R D S E R
M A S E R Y U J S L A M I N A
A L I U Q A X R T E T Y J K L
```

PUZZLE 65

1. How many cities of refuge were there to be altogether? (Numbers 35:6)

2. How many cities of refuge did Moses set up before the conquest of Canaan? (Deuteronomy 4:41-43)

3. How many of the cities of refuge were east of the Jordan? (Joshua 20:8)

4. Which tribe of Israel inherited the land containing the cities of Jericho and Jerusalem? (Joshua 18:21-28)

5. In the parable of the good Samaritan, the man who was robbed was going to _____ and was from _____ . (Luke 10:30)

6. The shortest sermon in the Bible consists of eight words: "Yet forty days and _____ shall be overthrown." To what city was that sermon preached? (Jonah 3:4)

7. When Naomi returned from afar with Ruth, to which city did they go? (Ruth 1:11-19)

8. To what city was Paul traveling when he was struck by the light of Jesus? (Acts 9:3-4)

9. In what city did Jesus speak to the woman at the well? (John 4:5-7)

10. What famous biblical city was also called "the city of palm trees"? (2 Chronicles 28:15)

11. What city was originally called Jebus? (Joshua 18:28)

12. What woman helped her son trick his father into giving him a blessing? (Genesis 27:1-17)

13. What woman tricked her father-in-law into doing his duty by her according to the levirate law? (Genesis 38:24-26)

14. The woman who gave birth to Moses and devised the plan to save his life was who? (Exodus 2:1-10; 6:20)

15. Who told the Israelites to be of good courage? (Deuteronomy 31:6)

16. Who told Joshua to be of good courage? (Joshua 1:9)

17. When Hezekiah told his army to be of good courage, what nation was coming after them? (2 Chronicles 32:7)

18. Which church did Paul, in his letter to that church, tell to be brave and strong? (1 Corinthians 16:13)

19. To which prophet was God speaking when He said He would make a new covenant with Israel and Judah? (Jeremiah 31:3)

20. God says that in His new covenant He will put His law where? (Jeremiah 31:33)

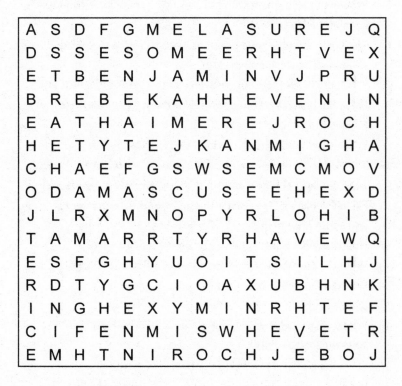

A	S	D	F	G	M	E	L	A	S	U	R	E	J	Q
D	S	S	E	S	O	M	E	E	R	H	T	V	E	X
E	T	B	E	N	J	A	M	I	N	V	J	P	R	U
B	R	E	B	E	K	A	H	H	E	V	E	N	I	N
E	A	T	H	A	I	M	E	R	E	J	R	O	C	H
H	E	T	Y	T	E	J	K	A	N	M	I	G	H	A
C	H	A	E	F	G	S	W	S	E	M	C	M	O	V
O	D	A	M	A	S	C	U	S	E	E	H	E	X	D
J	L	R	X	M	N	O	P	Y	R	L	O	H	I	B
T	A	M	A	R	R	T	Y	R	H	A	V	E	W	Q
E	S	F	G	H	Y	U	O	I	T	S	I	L	H	J
R	D	T	Y	G	C	I	O	A	X	U	B	H	N	K
I	N	G	H	E	X	Y	M	I	N	R	H	T	E	F
C	I	F	E	N	M	I	S	W	H	E	V	E	T	R
E	M	H	T	N	I	R	O	C	H	J	E	B	O	J

Puzzle 66

1. Upon what occasion did Jesus introduce the new covenant to His disciples? (Luke 22:20)

2. Hebrews 8:6 says the new covenant is more comprehensive, lasting, excellent, or strenuous.

3. Who is the mediator of the new covenant? (Hebrews 12:24)

4. Hebrews 13:20 says the new covenant is what?

5. Who made a covenant with his eyes never to look on a young woman? (Job 31:1)

6. The Lord said the heave offerings were a covenant of what common thing? (Numbers 18:19)

7. When did God create "the heaven and the earth"? (Genesis 1:1)

8. Fill in the blank: And the earth was without _____ , and void. (Genesis 1:2)

9. What is the Bible's first recorded word from God? (Genesis 1:3)

10. The "lights in the firmament of the heaven" were not marked by what passage of time, seasons, days, or months? (Genesis 1:14)

11. Fill in the blanks: "God made the beast of the earth after his _____ , and cattle after their _____ ."(Genesis 1:25)

12. How many days of creation were there? (Genesis 1:31)

13. What did God allow Adam and Eve to eat? (Genesis 1:29)

14. How did God describe everything that he had made? (Genesis 1:31)

15. What reason did God give for creating a companion for Adam? (Genesis 2:18)

16. Fill in the blanks: Moses told the Israelites that God was bringing them into a good land of _____ and _____ . (hint: not milk and honey) (Deuteronomy 8:8)

17. What was sown in the parable of the sower? (Matthew 13:3-4)

18. Who had a dream about seven heads of plump grain and seven heads of thin grain? (Genesis 41:5-7)

19. Fill in the blank: in describing the compassion of the Messiah, Isaiah says He will not quench the smoking _____ . (Isaiah 42:3)

20. Fill in the blank: In Matthew 13:24-30 Jesus tells the parable of the wheat and _____ .

```
A M T I U R F D N A S B R E H
L O N E L I N E S S A D O G H
K N P O Y R E A F R G E I N G
H T S E R A T R L W E E T I C
O H K N M W H E A T B S N N H
A S L D X I Y U P X D B E N V
R N I B A C A E V B N N L I M
A M E X L Q U I L F I B L G E
H E G D F U S A L T K Y E E S
P A N M X U Z E E Y O P C B V
B U R B S Z S A T W E D X E G
J O R E P P U S T S A L E H T
F U J T S A D F G K E D Y T I
E F D B E V E R L A S T I N G
I O D O O G Y R E V A D N I K
```

Puzzle 67

1. God told the Israelites that if they were disobedient their livestock would not what? (Deuteronomy 28:18)
2. Who cursed the day he was born? (Job 3:1)
3. When Shimei cursed David, what did David's captain call Shimei? A _____ _____ . (2 Samuel 16:9)
4. The curse of the Lord is on the house of whom? (Proverbs 3:33)
5. To whom did God say, "You are cursed more than all cattle, and more than every beast of the field"? (Genesis 3:14 NKJV)
6. Fill in the blank: Daniel _____ in his heart that he would not defile himself with the portion of the king's meat. (Daniel 1:8)
7. Melzar was set over Daniel and his friends by the prince of Babylon or eunuchs? (Daniel 1:11)
8. How many days did Daniel and his friends eat the food they requested as a test? (Daniel 1:15)
9. Fill in the blanks: God gave them _____ and skill in all learning and _____ . (Daniel 1:17)
10. Fill in the blank: Because Daniel interpreted Nebuchadnezzar's dream, Nebuchadnezzar made Daniel " _____ of the governors over all the wise men of Babylon." (Daniel 2:48)
11. Who was the king of Persia when Daniel was thrown into the lions' den? (Daniel 6:1, 16)
12. The people who tried to find fault in Daniel were magicians and sorcerers or presidents and princes? _____ and _____ .
13. Who said to Daniel, "Thy God whom thou servest continually, he will deliver thee"? (Daniel 6:16)
14. Fill in the blanks: The king's law was the law of the _____ and _____ . (Daniel 6:8)
15. Whom did God send to shut the lions' mouths? (Daniel 6:22)
16. How many times a day did Daniel kneel and pray? (Daniel 6:10)
17. Fill in the blank: Of those three daughters was it said, "In all the

land were found no women so beautiful as the daughters of _____?"
(Job 42:15 NKJV)

18. What was the name of Jacob's only daughter? (Genesis 30:20–21)

19. Of the four women Jacob had children with, which woman was the mother of his daughter? Leah, Rachel, Bilhah, or Zilpah? (Genesis 30:20–21)

20. Whose daughters helped him repair the walls of Jerusalem? (Nehemiah 3:12)

E	D	E	M	E	D	E	S	G	N	I	K	P	H	T
A	S	D	G	P	R	E	S	I	D	E	N	T	S	A
T	H	R	E	E	J	K	N	O	W	L	E	D	G	E
R	T	Y	U	R	P	I	O	D	C	V	B	B	N	W
M	A	E	H	S	C	H	I	E	F	V	O	C	I	H
U	S	D	A	I	J	R	N	S	O	J	I	C	R	P
L	E	G	N	A	C	E	V	O	H	J	K	Y	P	A
L	Q	U	I	N	T	N	E	P	R	E	S	E	S	U
A	K	L	D	S	B	I	E	R	D	M	O	P	F	X
H	D	E	A	F	S	H	C	U	N	U	E	T	F	Y
S	E	Q	U	H	I	R	T	P	W	I	S	D	O	M
A	D	U	A	Q	V	B	M	F	U	O	S	H	E	O
P	S	E	T	R	E	F	D	S	E	C	N	I	R	P
A	L	E	R	A	G	U	I	O	S	U	I	R	A	D
Y	E	D	R	G	O	D	D	A	E	D	J	O	B	S

PUZZLE 68

1. What Old Testament hero gave his daughter upper and lower springs as a wedding present? (Judges 1:15)

2. How many daughters did King Saul have? (1 Samuel 14:49)

3. Jesus was clothed in a garment that reached to His knees or feet? (Revelation 1:13)

4. Fill in the blank: He was standing in the middle of seven _____. (Revelation 1:13 NKJV)

5. Fill in the blank: His eyes were like a _____ of _____. (Revelation 1:14)

6. Fill in the blanks: His voice was like the _____ of _____. (Revelation 1:15)

7. Where were the seven stars located on him? (Revelation 1:16)

8. What went out of His mouth? A _____ two-edged _____. (Revelation 1:16)

9. What did John compare Jesus' countenance to? (Revelation 1:16)

10. Which three disciples were on the Mount of Transfiguration with Jesus? (Matthew 17:1–2)

11. When Jesus asked, "Who do you say that I am?" which disciple answered, "You are the Christ"? (Matthew 16:15–16 NKJV)

12. Which disciple brought his brother to Jesus? (John 1:40–41)

13. Which disciple was a tax collector before he followed Jesus? (Matthew 9:9)

14. Which of the following was not a fisherman when Jesus called him? Peter, Andrew, James, Nathanael. (Matthew 4:18–22; John 1:45–48)

15. Which disciple had Iscariot as part of his name? (Mark 3:19)

16. Which disciple demanded proof that Jesus had risen? (John 20:24–25)

17. How many disciples were at the cross when Jesus was crucified? (John 19:26)

18. Before he was a disciple of Jesus, who was Andrew a disciple of? (John 1:40)

19. Who said "Does the wild donkey bray when it has grass"? Bildad, Eliphaz, Job, or Zophar? (Job 6:5)

20. Which Gospel writer records the exact fulfillment of the prophecy that Jesus would ride on a colt? (Matthew 21:5)

```
S  T  J  U  I  O  S  D  J  G  H  T  L  E  R
A  S  S  O  U  N  D  D  A  U  Q  H  E  A  H
J  I  W  K  H  A  E  N  M  T  R  O  A  D  S
S  T  U  P  E  N  D  A  E  M  I  M  N  U  Y
E  P  U  F  O  I  R  F  S  A  B  A  A  E  V
C  A  L  E  B  D  O  N  M  T  I  S  H  S  U
E  B  R  E  T  A  W  N  R  T  A  H  T  D  N
X  E  R  T  W  U  S  K  L  H  E  R  A  N  U
S  H  I  N  M  P  L  S  W  E  R  D  N  A  S
C  T  R  E  N  M  K  L  I  W  O  R  P  T  E
G  N  S  A  D  U  J  R  S  Y  E  A  R  S  H
I  H  S  F  R  E  T  E  P  E  F  V  A  P  S
B  O  J  D  N  A  H  T  H  G  I  R  H  M  A
G  J  M  A  T  T  H  E  W  B  R  E  S  A  K
A  S  H  J  E  D  I  P  O  W  E  M  A  L  F
```

Puzzle 69

1. What apostle mentions Balaam and his donkey in the second book he wrote in the New Testament? (2 Peter 2:15-16)

2. When Samaria was under siege by Syria, how many shekels did a donkey's head sell for? (2 Kings 6:25)

3. In blessing his sons, which son did Jacob say was a strong donkey? (Genesis 49:14)

4. Which of the following is not associated with a dove? Moses, Noah, Jesus, or Jonah? (Genesis 8:9; Matthew 3:16; Jonah means "dove")

5. The psalmist say he would "fly away and _____ ,"if he had the wings of a dove. (Psalm 55:6)

6. Fill in the blank: Jesus said to be wise as _____ and harmless as doves. (Matthew 10:16)

7. Fill in the blank: Jacob dreamed of a _____ that went straight to heaven. (Genesis 28:10-12)

8. Fill in the blanks: Pharaoh dreamed that seven skinny _____ ate seven fat _____ . (Genesis 41:20)

9. Who saw a sheet full of creatures and was told to "rise and eat"? (Acts 10:9-13)

10. Who was warned in a dream not to go back to Herod? (Matthew 2:1, 12)

11. In Daniel's prophetic dream of kingdoms to come, how many beasts did Daniel see? (Daniel 7:3)

12. Who was told in a dream to take a wife, even though she was expecting a child? (Matthew 1:20)

13. Who was disturbed because she had a dream about Jesus? (Matthew 27:17-19)

14. Which son of King Saul did God protect by using an earthquake to keep the Philistines away? (1 Samuel 14:13-15)

15. Amos dates his words as how many years before the earthquake? (Amos 1:1)

16. Which apostle was in prison when an earthquake set him free? (Acts 16:25–26)
17. What man in the Bible is specifically referred to as "the Jews' enemy"? (Esther 3:10)
18. What enemy of Israel did King Saul fail to wipe out after God commanded him to? (1 Samuel 15:12–15)
19. What did Ruth glean in Boaz's field? (Ruth 2:17)
20. What evangelist had four daughters who prophesied? (Acts 21:8–9)

S	E	F	H	O	P	N	A	H	T	A	N	O	J	E
I	N	T	E	I	R	A	H	C	A	S	S	I	X	T
S	T	N	E	P	R	E	S	B	H	P	E	S	O	J
P	O	Y	F	L	U	A	S	N	O	J	S	Y	E	A
A	S	X	I	O	T	B	E	T	U	F	O	U	R	S
R	W	A	W	P	E	T	E	R	P	I	M	Y	U	T
A	W	T	S	Q	U	I	A	N	T	Y	E	R	O	R
I	S	D	E	O	P	K	L	C	E	C	V	B	N	E
C	A	T	T	L	A	D	O	L	I	P	A	Y	R	D
H	I	O	A	T	E	W	R	Y	I	H	G	T	E	D
E	F	G	L	E	R	A	T	N	A	M	A	H	S	A
A	F	V	I	N	B	M	I	G	T	Y	U	G	E	L
L	U	A	P	S	E	R	N	E	M	E	S	I	W	U
O	P	I	L	I	H	P	T	E	R	E	T	E	P	Y
W	E	R	I	S	E	T	I	K	E	L	A	M	A	P

Puzzle 70

1. Of what material was the ephod to be made? (Exodus 28:6)
2. What was the ephod? One of the high priest's _____ . (Exodus 28:4)
3. How many stones for the ephod were to be inscribed with the names of the tribes of Israel? (Exodus 28:9)
4. What were the ephod stones to be made of? (Exodus 28:9)
5. How many straps joined the ephod? (Exodus 28:7)
6. How were the tribes to be listed on the stones? In order of their _____ . (Exodus 28:10)
7. What type of setting were the stones to be in? (Exodus 28:11)
8. In what location were the stones to be attached to the ephod? (Exodus 28:12)
9. Were the braided chains on the ephod supposed to be made of silver or gold? (Exodus 28:14)
10. In Isaiah 9:6–7, what word follows "everlasting"?
11. Fill in the blank: Psalm 90:2 says that from everlasting to everlasting the Lord is __.
12. Fill in the blank: The eternal God is your refuge, and underneath are the everlasting _____ . (Deuteronomy 33:27)
13. Fill in the blank: John 3:16 says that whoever _____ in Him has everlasting life.
14. To whom did Paul say, "You judge yourselves unworthy of everlasting life"? (Acts 13:45–46)
15. Fill in the blank: To reap everlasting life, Paul says we must sow to the _____ . (Galatians 6:8)
16. Fill in the blank: Faith is the evidence of things _____ . (Hebrews 11:1)
17. Without faith it is impossible to do what? (Hebrews 11:6)
18. Who said he had fought the good fight and kept the faith? (2 Timothy 4:7)
19. Who shall live by faith? (Habakkuk 2:4)

20. About whom did Jesus say, "I have not found such great faith, not even in Israel"? (Matthew 8:8–10 NKJV)

```
A  E  P  T  Y  W  T  H  E  J  U  S  T  E  D
S  W  L  I  P  O  W  S  E  V  E  I  L  E  B
C  U  E  V  I  D  O  G  E  S  A  E  L  P  A
Y  U  A  P  W  E  O  A  R  H  J  K  I  G  H
A  C  S  W  E  L  I  R  U  M  N  O  N  Y  X
Q  T  E  U  D  F  P  M  U  I  B  C  E  N  M
U  I  G  F  A  T  H  E  R  I  G  N  N  M  C
I  R  O  N  I  O  E  N  R  Y  R  C  A  S  D
E  I  S  G  N  O  W  T  W  E  R  T  B  C  Z
E  P  N  M  O  P  H  S  N  E  E  S  T  O  N
A  S  C  E  N  T  U  R  I  O  N  T  Y  D  X
F  X  O  L  S  I  U  S  G  N  M  E  D  O  G
A  X  U  C  E  W  M  T  O  P  K  L  S  E  C
Z  A  G  A  S  R  E  D  L  U  O  H  S  H  Y
P  U  E  S  A  R  I  J  U  G  M  V  O  K  L
```

Puzzle 71

1. People worshipped their false gods at _____ . (2 Kings 17:29)

2. What princess of Sidon introduced Baal worship to Israel? (1 Kings 16:31–32)

3. Samson's death was in a temple to what god? (Judges 16:23)

4. Elijah slew 450 prophets of what god? (1 Kings 18:22, 40)

5. What king of Israel was the first to build places for the worship of Chemosh and Molech? (1 Kings 11:7)

6. What judge of Israel pulled down his own father's altar to Baal because God commanded him to? (Judges 6:24–25)

7. What king had Daniel thrown in the lions' den because Daniel refused to pray to him instead of praying to God? (Daniel 6:9–16)

8. Where did Abram go to escape a famine in his land? (Genesis 12:10)

9. Isaac escaped the famine in the land of the _____ ? (Genesis 26:1)

10. Who managed the store of provisions in Egypt during the seven-year famine? (Genesis 41:29–30, 56)

11. To what land did Naomi and her husband go to escape famine in Judah? (Ruth 1:1)

12. During David's reign a famine occurred that lasted how many years? (2 Samuel 21:1)

13. What king proclaimed a fast throughout all Judah before he inquired of the Lord? (2 Chronicles 20:3)

14. In the days of Nehemiah, the people fasted and repented and then read the Book of the what? (Nehemiah 9:1–3)

15. What did Jesus say hypocrites had to show they are fasting? A sad _____. (Matthew 6:16)

16. Which one of Abram's brothers was Lot's father? (Genesis 11:27)

17. Who was the father of Aaron, Miriam, and Moses? (Exodus 6:20)

18. Who was King Saul's father? (1 Samuel 9:1–2)

19. Who was called the father of all who dwell in tents and have livestock? (Genesis 4:20)

20. Who was David's father? (Ruth 4:17)

```
A S D J E R T Y L A B A J V C
T H R E E U I O P R T Y U W E
H O S H R I G E S B I G A M N
R W T O S E N I T S I L I H P
E E R S X C G T A D Y R E E B
Y F L H M O A B E T O L N C M
N O G A D X D O E P Y H A N R
S F U P X O N J P Y L N M A I
Z A P H I S V O N G M J L N B
H E D A R I U S L E B E Z E J
S S F T M E S E Y I U S M T R
I T E A S O U P I K L S F N G
K L R N A R A H D S E E K U L
W M F G T Y I H N O M O L O S
A E S E C A L P H G I H N C M
```

PUZZLE 72

1. The image Nebuchadnezzar erected on the plain of Dura was made of what? (Daniel 3:1)

2. Fill in the blank: Anytime the people heard music, they were to _____ the image. (Daniel 3:5)

3. Who told the king that Shadrach, Meshach, and Abednego refused to bow down and worship the image? (Daniel 3:8–12)

4. Who are the three people who said, "If it be so, our God whom we serve is able to deliver us from the burning fiery furnace, and he will deliver us out of thine hand, O king"? (Daniel 3:16–17)

5. Who was commanded to bind Shadrach, Meshach, and Abednego? (Daniel 3:20)

6. Fill in the blanks: The form of the fourth is like the _____ of _____ . (Daniel 3:25)

7. Who was the firstborn of David's brothers? (1 Samuel 16:6)

8. Who was the firstborn of Jacob's sons? (Genesis 35:23)

9. Who was the firstborn of David's sons? (2 Samuel 3:2)

10. Who was the firstborn of Joseph's sons, Ephraim or Manasseh? (Genesis 48:17–18)

11. Who was the firstborn, Rachel or Leah? (Genesis 29:18)

12. About whom is the Bible speaking in the following verse: "Through faith he kept the passover, and the sprinkling of blood, lest he that destroyed the firstborn should touch them." (Hebrews 11:24, 28)

13. Fill in the blank: Noah's story is recorded in the book of _____ .

14. Fill in the blank: In contrast to the wickedness of his generation, "Noah walked _____ _____ . (Genesis 6:9)

15. What are the names of Noah's three sons? (Genesis 5:32)

16. Fill in the blank: "Noah found _____ in the eyes of the Lord." (Genesis 6:8)

17. Once the flooding was over, the mountaintops could first be seen after how many months? (Genesis 8:5)

18. A dove released by Noah returned with what in her mouth to indicate she had found dry land? (Genesis 8:11)

19. What represents God's promise to never flood the earth again? (Genesis 9:12–13 NIV)

20. After the flood, what did Noah plant? (Genesis 9:20)

```
W  E  Y  U  E  L  H  T  E  H  P  A  J  I  K
X  M  A  H  E  S  S  A  N  A  M  R  O  P  L
A  S  R  A  Y  B  N  M  O  N  E  B  U  E  R
G  I  H  B  N  S  E  S  O  M  E  W  D  N  A
T  S  F  G  O  I  W  N  Z  M  E  L  U  E  D
Q  E  A  J  K  P  I  H  S  R  O  W  P  M  N
D  N  N  U  I  O  D  C  B  G  N  M  O  Y  W
R  E  G  D  C  H  T  A  D  Y  H  T  G  T  O
A  G  J  K  L  S  P  R  B  A  I  L  E  H  B
Y  W  I  T  H  G  O  D  E  N  A  I  N  G  N
E  K  N  E  M  R  H  A  V  B  O  R  D  I  I
N  I  M  Q  Y  A  X  H  C  A  H  S  E  M  A
I  O  D  P  L  C  Z  S  A  D  F  G  B  I  R
V  O  V  S  E  E  S  N  A  E  D  L  A  H  C
G  W  K  J  H  Y  F  A  E  L  E  V  I  L  O
```

Puzzle 73

1. Who was the first murderer? (Genesis 4:8)
2. Who was the first boat builder? (Genesis 6:15)
3. Who was the first disciple of Jesus? (John 1:40)
4. Who is the first queen mentioned in the Bible was queen of what country? (1 Kings 10:1)
5. Who was the first high priest of Israel? (Numbers 17:5, 8)
6. The first pharaoh mentioned in the Bible was associated with whom? (Genesis 12:15, 17)
7. What was the first miracle performed by Jesus? (John 2:9)
8. What is the first church mentioned in Revelation? (Revelation 2:1)
9. Who was the first shepherd? (Genesis 4:2)
10. Who was the first wife of David? (1 Samuel 18:27)
11. Who was the first man to build a city? (Genesis 4:17)
12. Who is the first priest mentioned in the Bible? (Genesis 14:18)
13. Who were the first people the children of Israel fought after they had left Egypt? (Exodus 17:8)
14. The altar someone would encounter when entering the tabernacle was made out of what metal? (Exodus 27:1–2 NIV)
15. Who built the first altar? (Genesis 8:20)
16. What was the first offering mentioned in the Bible? (Genesis 4:3)
17. What was the first thing God created? (Genesis 1:3)
18. Who was the first man who didn't die? (Genesis 5:24)
19. What was the first thing God told Adam to tend and keep? (Genesis 2:15)
20. Who was the first woman mentioned in the Bible after Eve? (Genesis 4:17)

```
A W E W H C O N E B N E M K L
O P A A R O N L P O I Z U R E
S D F T C E R T H E Y N O A H
C T H E G A R D E N B O M M U
X C V R T I I X S K R R K A Y
L J F I H A O N U B A B E H S
C A I N L S D F S T Y E D A R
L P O T I E U T I U R F E R H
W R T O E J B G U L V B Z B A
E F I W S N I A C B A X I A Z
R V L I G H T E B Y T H H S A
D I T N Y B M Q U I Y R C T V
N O S E T I K E L A M A L I W
A X D R E T R N H Y R T E N M
P I U Q W E R U Y T P O M L K
```

Puzzle 74

1. What was the first plague of Egypt? (Exodus 7:14–25)

2. On what day of creation did God create flowers and plants? (Genesis 1:12–13)

3. What flower did Jesus say was better arrayed than Solomon in all his glory? (Matthew 6:28–29)

4. Fill in the blank: One of the flowers mentioned in the Bible is the rose of _____ . (Song of Solomon 2:1)

5. Isaiah says, "The grass withers and the flowers fall," but what endures forever? (Isaiah 40:6–8 NIV)

6. What plants did Moses' mother hide him among? (Exodus 2:3 NKJV)

7. Hyssop was used to apply _____ and the water of purification. (Leviticus 14:1–7; Numbers 19:1–19)

8. Fill in the blanks: And forgive us our _____ as we forgive our _____ . (Matthew 6:12)

9. God said that if His people humble themselves and pray, He will heal their what? (2 Chronicles 7:14)

10. Fill in the blank: The psalmist said the Lord is good and _____ to forgive. (Psalm 86:5)

11. What book of the Bible is this verse from: "I do not say to you, up to seven times, but up to seventy times seven"? (Matthew 18:22 NKJV)

12. Fill in the blanks: If we confess our sins, He is _____ and _____ to forgive us our sins. (1 John 1:9)

13. Who was called the friend of God? (James 2:23)

14. Who was David's good friend? (1 Samuel 18:1)

15. Fill in the blanks: Proverbs 17:17 says a friend loves at _____ _____ .

16. Which two people said to Jesus, "He whom you love is sick"? (John 11:1–3 NKJV)

17. From what city did Paul escape when his friends let him down over the wall in a huge basket? (Acts 9:22–25)

18. What three disciples comprised Jesus' inner circle? (Matthew 17:1)

19. Fill in the blank: Can two walk together except they be _____ ? (Amos 3:3)

20. The name of the forbidden tree was the Knowledge of _____ and _____ ? (Genesis 2:9)

```
A  W  R  S  E  F  T  S  R  O  T  B  E  D  B
O  D  L  E  I  F  E  H  T  F  O  Y  L  I  L
H  R  E  H  Y  D  N  A  L  A  S  F  H  U  O
S  I  J  S  M  N  E  R  E  A  D  Y  O  D  O
E  H  T  U  J  A  W  O  R  D  O  F  G  O  D
M  T  E  R  S  H  M  N  I  N  H  O  J  O  K
A  D  I  L  C  T  H  Y  K  U  P  T  L  L  E
J  L  F  U  V  A  B  E  V  I  L  D  E  B  C
E  U  D  B  Q  N  T  A  H  T  R  A  M  O  M
R  F  O  L  K  O  Y  T  R  E  D  E  B  T  S
E  H  O  R  T  J  A  F  V  B  I  R  E  R  Y
T  T  G  U  J  S  U  C  S  A  M  A  D  E  R
E  I  P  A  G  R  E  E  D  L  J  U  H  T  A
P  A  B  R  A  H  A  M  W  E  H  T  T  A  M
D  F  O  Z  X  S  E  M  I  T  L  L  A  W  E
```

Puzzle 75

1. What tree stood near the forbidden tree? (Genesis 2:9)

2. God banished Adam and Eve from the garden to prevent them from what? (Genesis 3:22)

3. When God cursed the ground, what two things did He say it would bring forth? (Genesis 3:17–18)

4. What job was given to cherubim after the expulsion of Adam and Eve from Eden? (Genesis 3:24)

5. Fill in the blank: Ezekiel called the Garden of Eden the Garden of _____ . (Ezekiel 28:13)

6. Fill in the blank: The virtuous woman is said to have a price above what? (Proverbs 31:10)

7. Which of the following is NOT a gemstone found on the breastplate of the high priest: sapphire, turquoise, amethyst, or garnet? (Exodus 28:17–21 NKJV)

8. How many gems were on the high priest's breastplate? (Exodus 28:21)

9. The list of gems in Ezekiel 28 was associated with what place? (Ezekiel 28:13)

10. How many layers of gemstones make up the foundation of the new Jerusalem? (Revelation 21:19–20)

11. Matthew's genealogy of Jesus begins with which most ancient individual? (Matthew 1:2)

12. Each group of Matthew's genealogy of Jesus has how many generations? (Matthew 1:17)

13. Luke's genealogy of Jesus traces Jesus' ancestors back to whom? (Luke 3:38)

14. Whom did Paul urge not to give heed to fables and endless genealogies? (1 Timothy 1:4)

15. Who is the only woman mentioned in both Jesus' genealogy and God's Hall of Fame? (Matthew 1:5; Hebrews 11:31)

16. Where is the first genealogy listed in the Bible? (Genesis 5)

17. The genealogy in the previous question starts with whom and ends with whom?

18. Upon what mountain did Elijah defeat the prophets of Baal? (1 Kings 18:19)

19. What patriarch went out not knowing where he went? (Hebrews 11:8)

20. When God told Jonah to go to Nineveh, to what city did Jonah try to flee? (Jonah 1:3)

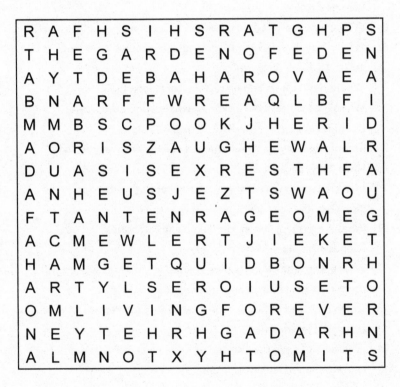

```
R A F H S I H S R A T G H P S
T H E G A R D E N O F E D E N
A Y T D E B A H A R O V A E A
B N A R F F W R E A Q L B F I
M M B S C P O O K J H E R I D
A O R I S Z A U G H E W A L R
D U A S I S E X R E S T H F A
A N H E U S J E Z T S W A O U
F T A N T E N R A G E O M E G
A C M E W L E R T J I E K E T
H A M G E T Q U I D B O N R H
A R T Y L S E R O I U S E T O
O M L I V I N G F O R E V E R
N E Y T E H R H G A D A R H N
A L M N O T X Y H T O M I T S
```

Puzzle 76

1. Abram's point of origin was Ur of the _____? (Genesis 11:31 NKJV)
2. Moses sent the twelve spies into the Promised Land from the Wilderness of where? (Numbers 13:3)
3. From what city did Samson carry off the gates after the Philistines tried to lock him in? (Judges 16:1–3)
4. At what site did the Lord confound the language of the earth? (Genesis 11:9)
5. Where was Ezekiel when he began to prophesy? (Ezekiel 1:3 NIV)
6. Where was the garden of Gethsemane located? (Matthew 26:30–36; Mark 14:26–32)
7. Where did Lazarus and his sisters live? (John 11:1)
8. When Moses fled from Egypt, to what country did he go? (Exodus 2:15)
9. Out of what city was Paul lowered in a basket over the wall? (Acts 9:19–25)
10. What gate in Jerusalem was the Pool of Bethesda near? (John 5:2–4)
11. What are Pishon, Gihon, Hiddekel, and Euphrates? (Genesis 2:10–14 NKJV)
12. Where were the two disciples headed when Jesus walked with them after His resurrection? (Luke 24:13)
13. Toward the end of his life, Jeremiah was taken captive to what country? (Jeremiah 43:7–8)
14. Where was Eve in the Garden of Eden when the serpent spoke to her? (Genesis 2:9; 3:6)
15. Where was Adam when the serpent spoke to Eve? (Genesis 3:6)
16. What was the "great city," or capital, of Assyria? (Genesis 10:11–12 NIV; Jonah 3:3)
17. From what mountain was Moses given a look into the Promised Land? (Deuteronomy 32:48–49)

18. When Moses died, in what land did God bury him? (Deuteronomy 34:6)
19. Where did Paul meet Aquila and Priscilla? (Acts 18:1–2)
20. Of what significance was Mount Hor to Aaron? (Numbers 20:25–28)

```
G  C  A  B  S  T  E  R  I  V  E  R  S  Y  E
O  E  S  E  V  I  L  O  F  O  T  N  U  O  M
U  N  I  T  N  I  N  E  V  E  H  E  C  A  M
A  T  R  H  E  T  A  G  P  E  E  H  S  U  A
W  E  N  A  I  D  I  M  B  N  G  C  A  G  U
R  R  O  N  W  S  T  A  G  L  Y  L  M  H  S
E  F  O  Y  G  R  W  A  A  K  P  Y  A  S  M
H  Y  B  T  R  E  V  I  O  U  T  L  D  N  Q
E  G  E  H  R  E  R  M  N  A  Y  E  M  A  U
D  O  N  I  N  U  T  R  I  U  Y  B  T  E  I
I  B  T  I  B  R  T  Y  M  N  K  A  L  D  O
S  I  N  T  Y  N  O  L  Y  B  A  B  Z  L  E
E  F  U  G  H  J  K  L  E  W  N  A  R  A  P
B  C  O  R  I  N  T  H  G  E  J  K  L  H  G
O  I  M  B  A  O  M  F  O  D  N  A  L  C  A
```

Puzzle 77

1. To what city did Jesus lead His disciples just before His ascension? (Luke 24:50-51)

2. What did Abraham name the place where God told him to sacrifice Isaac? (Genesis 22:14)

3. Second Samuel 21:22 said there were four born to the giant where?

4. Gideon's story is found in what book of the Bible?

5. Fill in the blank: The angel of the Lord who appeared to Gideon said, "The Lord is with you, mighty _____ ." (Judges 6:12 NIV)

6. Fill in the blanks: Gideon said that he was of the _____ clan in Manasseh, and he was the _____ in his family. (Judges 6:15 NKJV)

7. Fill in the blanks: Gideon was told to destroy his father's altar to _____ and cut down the Asherah _____ . (Judges 6:25 NIV)

8. Fill in the blank: the Israelite battle cry was "A sword for the Lord and for _____ !" (Judges 7:20)

9. Fill in the blank: The gifts the people gave to Aaron for his use as high priest became _____ gifts. (Exodus 28:38)

10. When Elisha refused to take gifts from Naaman, who took the gifts? (2 Kings 5:20)

11. The queen of what country brought Solomon spices, gold, and precious stones? (1 Kings 10:1-2)

12. Who gave Jesus a gift of very costly perfume? (John 12:2-3)

13. On the Feast of Purim, the Jews gave gifts to whom? (Esther 9:22)

14. James 1:17 says every good gift comes from where? (James 1:17)

15. Fill in the blank: Every man is a _____ to one who gives gifts. (Proverbs 19:6)

16. Fill in the blanks: The Bible says that even _____ people know how to give _____ gifts. (Matthew 7:11)

17. Once every year Solomon received tribute from Tarshish that included what animals? (1 Kings 10:22-23)

18. In Peter's sermon on the day of Pentecost, he offered those who repented and were baptized in Christ's name the gift of the what? (Acts 2:38)

19. Which gift did Paul say the church at Corinth was misusing? (1 Corinthians 14:2)

20. Fill in the blank: God is not the author of _____ but of peace. (1 Corinthians 14:33)

```
E R B T I R I P S Y L O H E S
C O N F U S I O N M V I B T E
U S K C O C A E P S D F V H U
O Y T R E D F G H A B O V E G
G L L K R Y X I B P N M F P N
L O P U I R Z Y R E S A G O O
M H O N B A D W E S T Y U O T
A Y S D H M V B B D N E I R F
S N L E A S T U N R L I K F J
I A G N G M C V O O P A C D E
D H E H R D T H E I O N A A V
F T P O T I U U D R L T R B A
J E H O V A H J I R E H N E M
P B I U Y T G R A A X C H K
S D F T S E K A E W J L E S T
```

Puzzle 78

1. Fill in the blank: Paul said he preferred the church would _____ rather than speak in tongues. (1 Corinthians 14:5)

2. Fill in the blank: Paul wrote to the Romans: "We have different gifts, according to the _____ given to each of us." (Romans 12:6 NIV)

3. According to Paul, those blessed with the gift of generosity should give with what? (Romans 12:8)

4. Fill in the blanks: Paul told the Romans those with the gift of prophecy should prophecy "according to the _____ of _____ . (Romans 12:6)

5. To what church did Paul send these words: "But one and the same Spirit works all these things, distributing to each one individually as He wills"? (1 Corinthians 12:11 NKJV)

6. According to Paul, what is the supreme gift of the Spirit to believers? (1 Corinthians 12:31; 13:13)

7. Psalm 19:1 says, "the _____ declare the glory of God."

8. When the tabernacle was finished and the glory of the Lord filled it, who could enter the tabernacle? (Exodus 40:35)

9. Fill in the blanks: The glory of the Lord departed from Israel when the _____ of the _____ was taken. (1 Samuel 4:17, 22)

10. According to 1 Chronicles 16:24, we are to declare the Lord's glory to whom?

11. "For all have sinned, and come short of the glory of God" is found in what book of the Bible? (Romans 3:23)

12. Fill in the blanks: John says the people who saw Jesus beheld His glory, which was full of _____ and _____ . (John 1:14)

13. The last part of the Lord's Prayer says God's glory is what? (Matthew 6:13)

14. Psalm 24 says that God is the _____ of the glory. (Psalm 24:10)

15. Of whom does the Bible say, "In all this _____ sinned not, nor charged God foolishly"? (Job 1:22)

16. About whom is the Bible speaking when it says that among men whose thoughts were only evil continually, this person found grace in the eyes of the Lord? (Genesis 6:5, 8)

17. About whom was God speaking when he said, "He has a different spirit in him and has followed Me fully"? (Numbers 14:24 NKJV)

18. Which of the following is not listed by name in Hebrews 11: Abel, Joseph, Rahab, or Elijah?

19. About whom of Noah's ancestors does the Bible say he "walked with God" and "God took him"? (Genesis 5:24)

20. What animal did Abraham sacrifice instead of his son Isaac? (Genesis 22:13)

E	R	Y	U	O	K	N	E	H	T	A	E	H	J	I
C	V	H	C	O	N	E	T	Q	W	M	R	R	G	K
A	S	D	F	H	J	K	L	C	A	L	E	B	R	T
F	O	R	E	V	E	R	A	R	S	B	R	P	H	J
A	G	F	H	J	P	Z	C	V	N	O	O	N	E	H
Y	U	H	I	K	R	A	E	X	E	C	M	J	N	A
S	D	A	E	C	O	Y	X	C	V	A	A	W	I	J
D	F	O	X	V	P	M	S	B	A	V	N	O	M	I
H	T	N	I	R	O	C	T	E	E	R	S	G	U	L
A	R	D	F	G	R	L	N	M	H	I	G	N	H	E
T	U	Y	T	Y	T	I	C	I	L	P	M	I	S	C
L	T	K	H	T	I	A	F	T	R	D	O	K	G	H
A	H	S	D	R	O	N	M	E	E	C	A	R	G	A
M	C	O	V	E	N	A	N	T	N	R	E	Y	P	T
A	S	D	T	Y	U	K	L	E	W	E	R	T	Y	U

Puzzle 79

1. How many years did Noah spend preparing the ark as God told Him? (Genesis 5:32; 7:11)

2. What prophet who devoutly feared God hid one hundred prophets from Jezebel? (1 Kings 18:3-4)

3. Who are the only two women mentioned in Hebrews 11? (verses 11, 31)

4. How many judges from the book of Judges are listed in Hebrews 11? (verse 32)

5. Who was the first person mentioned in the Hebrews 11 list? (verse 4)

6. Who was the last person mentioned by name in Hebrews 11? (verse 32)

7. Who has the most written about him in Hebrews 11?

8. Fill in the blank: In Hebrews 11 God said the world was not _____ of these. (verse 38)

9. How many people are mentioned by name in Hebrews 11?

10. In Matthew 5:17, what did Jesus say He came to do to the Law and the Prophets?

11. Numbers 32:23 says that if you _____ you will be _____ _____ .

12. Jesus says in John 14:15 that keeping God's _____ is proof of _____ Him.

13. What did God, through His prophet Samuel, say is "better than sacrifice"? (1 Samuel 15:22)

14. Fill in the blanks: Thou shalt love the Lord thy God with all thy _____ , and with all thy _____ , and with all thy _____ . (Matthew 22:37)

15. Fill in the blanks: Thou shalt love thy _____ as _____ . (Matthew 22:39)

16. Fill in the blank: Thou shalt have no other _____ before me. (Exodus 20:3)

17. How many days are we to labor? (Exodus 20:9)

18. What is the first thing listed that we should not covet, per the Ten Commandments? (Exodus 20:17)
19. According to Psalm 19, what of the Lord's are true and righteous? (Psalm 19:9)
20. What kind of stone were the Israelites not to use when building an altar? (Exodus 20:25)

J	E	S	U	O	H	S	R	O	B	H	G	I	E	N
G	A	F	O	U	N	D	H	J	K	L	R	T	I	Z
N	T	E	A	T	R	T	Y	U	L	U	O	S	R	C
H	E	W	N	J	E	C	N	E	I	D	E	B	O	N
E	R	T	A	F	L	E	S	Y	H	T	J	H	D	X
F	G	H	J	K	L	Y	E	W	R	T	A	B	E	L
O	S	D	O	G	P	A	B	R	A	H	A	M	R	Y
S	T	E	N	N	T	R	A	E	H	G	H	I	D	H
D	N	Y	E	I	F	R	E	S	A	T	M	N	N	T
T	E	V	E	V	B	A	H	A	R	L	K	D	U	R
Z	M	A	T	O	E	Y	O	B	A	D	I	A	H	O
X	G	O	X	L	E	U	M	A	S	N	M	G	E	W
I	D	T	I	R	E	R	O	B	H	G	I	E	N	F
S	U	C	S	T	N	E	M	D	N	A	M	M	O	C
K	J	E	T	M	E	H	T	L	L	I	F	L	U	F

Puzzle 80

1. Where did Moses tell the Israelites they were to write God's commandments? (Deuteronomy 6:9)

2. According to Paul, the curse that Christ has redeemed us from is the curse of what? (Galatians 3:13)

3. To what food does Psalm 19 compare God's law? (Psalm 19:7-10)

4. Galatians 6:2 say we are to _____ one another's _____ to fulfill the law of Christ.

5. God promises in Isaiah 58:13-14 that those who keep the _____ will find _____ in the Lord.

6. Joshua 1:8 says that if we meditate on the Book of the Law day and night, we will have a _____ way and good _____ .

7. For whom does Paul say the law is not intended? (1 Timothy 1:9)

8. Fill in the blanks: Because Rahab believed in God and hid the Israelites spies, God told her she would not perish in _____ if she bound a _____ thread in her window. (Joshua 2:18)

9. How many stones did David take out of the brook when he went to fight Goliath? (1 Samuel 17:40)

10. Shamgar was a judge of Israel who used what to slay six hundred Philistines? (Judges 3:31)

11. To show that Aaron was His choice for high priest, God made Aaron's rod what? (Numbers 17:1-8)

12. Samson used a donkey's what to slay a thousand of Israel's enemies? (Judges 15:16)

13. When a prophet's widow needed money to save her sons, Elisha multiplied her last pot of what? (2 Kings 4:1-7)

14. When Jesus needed to pay the temple tax, He directed Peter to find a coin in the mouth of a what? (Matthew 17:24-27)

15. When the poor widow gave her two mites, she gave _____ . (Mark 12:42-44)

16. When Moses asked the people to bring offerings for the making of the tabernacle, they brought gold _____ , _____ , and _____ . (Exodus 35:5, 21-22)

17. When Elisha succeeded Elijah, what did he receive of Elijah's as a symbol of his succession? (2 Kings 2:9-13)

18. In Psalm 119 each verse contains a reference to God's Word as His what? (Psalm 119:1)

19. In the parable of the sower, the Word of God is likened to what? (Luke 8:11)

20. In the list of the armor of God in Ephesians 6, the Word of God is the what? (Ephesians 6:17)

```
S G S G N I R R A E T Y U J I
A E L K H G N I H T Y R E V E
B D E E S Y U W E L T N A M A
B B R A C E L E T S H J N O P
A S D R T Y U A D R O W S I L
T E L R A C S A W K N H S I F
H M O S S O L B J A W B O N E
R T Y J S U I O E C V D N M P
S U O R E P S O R P E A Y F R
N Y E R C T Y F I V E O N W A
E P O J C T D Z C Y G G X A E
D A S D U C V B H N M X O L B
R I N G S R E S O U H O N E Y
U S T S O P R O O D R I E H T
B U S U O E T H G I R E H T E
```

Puzzle 81

1. Which Gospel begins by saying the Word was in the beginning with God and was God?

2. Hebrews 4:12 says the Word of God is _____ , _____ , and _____ than a two-edged sword.

3. Jeremiah 23:29 says the Word of God is like a _____ and a _____ .

4. Hebrews 11:3 says something was framed by the Word of God. What was it?

5. Psalm 119:105 says the Word of God is a what?

6. The Bible says that the Word became flesh and _____ among us. (John 1:14)

7. God said that when His Word goes out, it will not return _____ . (Isaiah 55:11)

8. Fill in the blank: Ephesians 2:8 says grace is the _____ of God. (Ephesians 2:8)

9. To whom was Paul speaking when he said grace came through the kindness and love of God? (Titus 3:4, 7)

10. Who found grace in the eyes of the Lord? (Genesis 6:8)

11. Who became strong in spirit, filled with wisdom, and the grace of God was upon him? (Luke 2:40)

12. Fill in the blank: John said Jesus was full of grace and _____ . (John 1:14)

13. In Acts 4:33, who was great grace upon?

14. Fill in the blanks: Grace allows us to "serve God acceptably with reverence and _____ _____ ." (Hebrews 12:28 NKJV)

15. Fill in the blank: Peter tells us to grow in grace and _____ of our Lord and Savior Jesus Christ. (2 Peter 3:18)

16. In Genesis 8:22, who said "While the earth remains, seedtime and harvest. . .shall not cease"?

17. What book of the Bible contains this verse: "A time to plant, and a time to pluck what is planted"?

18. Fill in the blank: "The harvest is past, the summer is ended, and we are not _____ !" (Jeremiah 8:20 NKJV)

19. Who said, "The harvest truly is plentiful, but the laborers are few"? (Matthew 9:37 NKJV)

20. We are to ask the Lord of the harvest to send out whom? (Matthew 9:38)

```
W  T  J  E  R  T  Y  U  I  O  P  L  K  J  S
G  H  O  K  C  I  U  Q  R  E  P  R  A  H  S
T  E  H  S  E  T  S  A  I  S  E  L  C  C  E
Y  W  N  O  V  I  R  A  E  F  Y  L  D  O  G
T  O  R  P  O  W  E  R  F  U  L  E  Y  U  D
A  R  T  F  I  G  N  T  I  T  U  S  I  L  E
S  L  Y  U  D  E  O  A  R  E  M  M  A  H  L
A  D  W  E  L  T  A  J  E  G  H  M  I  K  W
S  S  E  C  V  G  H  E  N  B  P  N  M  L  O
U  X  C  F  O  R  Y  S  U  P  O  J  K  L  N
S  I  S  D  A  T  R  U  T  H  E  F  N  M  K
E  H  G  D  F  E  R  S  E  L  T  S  O  P  A
J  O  I  U  Y  G  O  D  L  Y  F  E  A  P  S
P  S  A  V  E  D  U  Y  T  R  E  S  D  F  G
A  S  F  H  G  F  S  R  E  R  O  B  A  L  E
```

PUZZLE 82

1. Fill in the blank: The fields are already _____ for harvest. (John 4:35)

2. Fill in the blanks: In order to be healed, Naaman had to _____ in the River _____ . (2 Kings 5:10)

3. About whom was Moses speaking when he said, "Please heal her, O God, I pray!" (Numbers 12:10–13 NKJV)

4. Which disciple had a mother-in-law whom Jesus healed? (Matthew 8:14–15)

5. What was the name of the pool where Jesus healed the paralyzed man? (John 5:2)

6. What people provoked God to the point where He said the fire of His anger would burn in the lowest hell? (Deuteronomy 32:21–23)

7. Who said, "Hell is naked before Him"? (Job 26:6)

8. Who said, "The wicked shall be turned into hell"? (Psalm 9:17 NKJV)

9. The psalmist said God is with us even in _____ . (Psalm 139:8)

10. Whose house does Proverbs say is the way to hell? (Proverbs 7:5, 27 NKJV)

11. The Bible says hell has _____ . (Matthew 16:18)

12. Fill in the blank: Mark 9:44 says that in hell the _____ never dies and _____ is never quenched.

13. Of whom was David speaking in Psalm 16:10 when he said, "You will not leave my soul in hell"?

14. The Bible says that hell has _____ . (Revelation 1:18)

15. Fill in the blank: When death and hell are cast into the lake of fire, the apostle John says this is the second _____ . (Revelation 20:14)

16. Whose wife was turned into a pillar of salt? (Genesis 19:26)

17. When a conqueror wanted to ruin the place he conquered, he sowed the land with _____ . (Judges 9:45)

18. Which two Gospels say the women brought spices to Jesus'
    tomb? (Mark 16:1; Luke 24:1)
19. What feast was associated with bitter herbs? (Exodus 12:8)
20. The writer of Song of Solomon compares his spouse to what when
    he lists the following spices: saffron, cinnamon, and frankincense?
    (Song of Solomon 4:12–14)

```
A T E K U L B R T F U I O L K
E M I R I A M B D I V A D F A
A B C V S J O K R R R E T E P
P E T O R J L U J E S U S N E
D T L E A L W Q U I N M T A C
M H A T E U H I S T O L E M X
R E S H L R T E H N A D R O J
O S V B I N A M L E T I H W K
W D A K T S E R T Y U H A L K
G A Y T E R D V C N M S N A J
G A T E S Y E R U Y H C F R A
D G O P U Y S T D C V B N O M
A P A S S O V E R R E T Y M M
L K I U Y T R Q W E K R A M D
A N E D R A G F J H R E T I W
```

Puzzle 83

1. What spice mixed with wine was offered to Jesus on the cross? (Mark 15:23)

2. What spicy herb did the complaining Israelites recall from their years of slavery in Egypt? (Numbers 11:4-8)

3. When Herod was harassing the church, which of Jesus' disciples did he kill with a sword? (Acts 12:1-2)

4. Who was the woman in Herod's life? (Mark 6:17)

5. What was the occasion when Herod agreed to behead John the Baptist? (Matthew 14:6)

6. Whose daughter actually asked for John the Baptist to be beheaded? (Matthew 14:6-8)

7. What was Herod's title as a ruler? (Luke 3:1 NKJV)

8. What shepherd was God speaking to when He said, "The place where you stand is holy ground"? (Exodus 3:5 NKJV)

9. Which of the Ten Commandments contains the word *holy*? (Exodus 20:8)

10. In order to be able to distinguish between holy and unholy things, what were the Israelites NOT to do when they went into the tabernacle? (Leviticus 10:9)

11. Fill in the blank: Psalm 48:1 says God is greatly to be praised in His holy _____ .

12. Fill in the blank: Hebrews 9:24 says that Christ has not entered holy places made with _____ .

13. In Genesis 1:2, the Spirit of the Lord was moving on the face of what?

14. Who tried to buy the gifts of the Holy Spirit? (Acts 8:18-19)

15. What name did Jesus use for the Holy Spirit in the KJV? (John 15:26)

16. On what New Testament occasion were the Holy Spirit, God the Father, and Jesus all present at the same time? (Matthew 3:16-17)

17. The Holy Spirit bears witness that we are God's what? (Romans 8:16)

18. What are the five symbols of the Holy Spirit? (John 7:38-39; John 3:8; Ephesians 1:13; Matthew 3:16; Acts 2:3)

19. According to the prophet Joel, the Holy Spirit enables young men and young women to see _____ and _____ ? (Joel 2:28-32; Acts 2:16-21)

```
A  T  R  F  U  I  Y  E  S  D  N  A  H  N  R
H  E  R  O  D  I  A  S  D  F  G  F  I  R  E
A  T  R  U  H  J  D  K  L  E  H  U  Y  E  T
S  R  N  R  L  O  H  P  C  I  L  R  A  G  A
S  A  E  T  W  A  T  E  R  S  E  A  R  E  W
E  R  R  H  I  U  R  O  B  T  M  E  V  Y  N
F  C  D  A  N  X  I  D  R  R  Y  O  U  J  M
V  H  L  Z  D  J  B  O  R  E  D  L  E  S  V
I  F  I  A  T  A  F  Y  L  U  A  P  U  A  K
S  T  H  E  A  M  U  B  N  M  N  O  M  I  S
I  Y  C  L  O  E  N  I  W  K  N  I  R  D  B
O  E  A  C  A  S  E  S  O  M  I  X  C  O  V
N  E  M  O  U  N  T  A  I  N  F  J  K  R  E
S  T  R  M  S  I  T  P  A  B  S  U  S  E  J
S  A  T  Y  S  E  H  P  O  R  P  E  I  H  E
```

Puzzle 84

1. According to Paul, we will not fulfill the _____ of the _____ if we walk in the Spirit. (Galatians 5:16)

2. According to Romans 8:26, the Holy Spirit does what for us?

3. What three things did Paul tell Timothy that God has given us, as opposed to a spirit of fear? (2 Timothy 1:7)

4. According to Paul, the four things the Holy Spirit-inspired scriptures describes as profitable are doctrine, _____ , correction, and _____ in righteousness. (2 Timothy 3:16)

5. There is a story in the Bible about _____ in a lion's carcass. (Judges 14:8)

6. The psalmist says the _____ of the _____ is sweeter than honey and the _____ . (Psalm 19:7-10)

7. The _____ Land was flowing with milk and honey. (Exodus 3:8)

8. _____ tasted like honey. (Exodus 16:31)

9. Honey was not to be used in any offering made by _____ . (Leviticus 2:11)

10. The song of Moses in Deuteronomy 32 says God would draw honey from what? (Deuteronomy 32:13)

11. When King Saul commanded his hungry army not to eat some honey they found, who ate it anyway? (1 Samuel 14:25-29)

12. Fill in the blank: Honey drips from the _____ of an immoral woman. (Proverbs 5:3)

13. Proverbs 16:24 says what kind of words are like honeycomb?

14. God commanded Ezekiel to eat a what that Ezekiel said tasted like honey in sweetness? (Ezekiel 3:3 NIV)

15. Who was described as eating locusts and wild honey? (Matthew 3:4)

16. What did the apostle John eat that was as sweet as honey in his mouth but made his stomach bitter? (Revelation 10:9)

17. "Honor thy father and mother" is the first commandment to contain a what? (Ephesians 6:1–3)
18. Who is without honor in his own country? (Matthew 13:57)
19. In addition to honor, the living creatures in heaven give _____ and _____ to Him who sits on the throne. (Revelation 4:9)
20. Fill in the blank: Psalm 96:6 says honor and _____ are before the Lord.

```
Y T S E J A M O S K N A H T P
R E R H O N E Y C O M B A P L
O T E H P O R P B A D M U L T
L D E Y T I E P N L R A J E K
G N O S E T S N B W O N N A Q
F I R E U C I L Y D L N A S K
A M S D R U M L I E O A H A O
H D R E P R O O F S L V T N O
W N H C U T R R E I Q K A T B
A U K R M S P C P M C V N X E
L O V E L N R S T O Y E O X L
G S A T J I T Y R R E S J T T
J O H N T H E B A P T I S T T
R T Y I P O W E R A S U R B I
Y E N O H E A H S E L F K M L
```

Puzzle 85

1. Fill in the blank: Proverbs 15:33 says that before honor is _____ .

2. Fill in the blank: According to Peter, we are to honor all _____ . (1 Peter 2:17 NKJV)

3. Fill in the blank: For surely there is a _____ and your hope will not be cut off. (Proverbs 23:18 NKJV)

4. There is more hope for a _____ than a man _____ in his own eyes. (Proverbs 26:12)

5. It is good that one should hope and wait quietly for the _____ of the _____ . (Lamentations 3:26)

6. Fill in the blank: Paul said hope does not _____ . (Romans 5:5 NKJV)

7. Fill in the blank: Hope that is _____ is not hope. (Romans 8:24)

8. Fill in the blank: Paul's definition of hope is "eagerly awaiting with _____ ." (Romans 8:25 NKJV)

9. Fill in the blank: Christ in you, the hope of _____ . (Colossians 1:27)

10. Paul says we are to wear the hope of salvation as a what? (1 Thessalonians 5:8)

11. Fill in the blank: Peter says our hope is a _____ hope. (1 Peter 1:3 NKJV)

12. To whom was the prophet Nathan speaking when he pointed out this king's sin with the words, "Thou art the man"? (2 Samuel 12:7)

13. Jesus told Peter that he would deny Him three times before the cock crowed how many times? (Mark 14:72)

14. When Miriam spoke against Moses, she was struck with leprosy for how many days? (Numbers 12:1–2, 14–15)

15. Who thought the king was going to honor him and instead ended up having to honor his worst enemy? (Esther 6:6–11)

16. When Elisha's servant lied to Naaman and took gifts from him, the servant was struck with what? (2 Kings 5:20–27)

17. When Nebuchadnezzar claimed glory instead of giving the glory to God, he became mad and lived like a wild what? (Daniel 4:24–25, 30–33)

18. When Herod allowed the people to say that his voice was the voice of a god, the angel of the Lord struck him what? (Acts 12:20–23)

19. Isaac met who because Abraham's servant brought her to meet him? (Genesis 24:64–65)

20. Who was Bathsheba's first husband? (2 Samuel 11:3)

E	L	A	M	I	N	A	R	T	D	Y	U	I	V	B
A	N	I	K	L	N	O	I	T	A	V	L	A	S	A
S	A	R	T	Y	D	G	U	O	V	P	O	L	M	B
S	M	F	G	G	N	E	K	U	I	Y	R	T	E	H
D	A	T	R	I	T	Y	A	U	D	A	D	W	M	A
H	H	N	V	E	F	O	P	D	I	J	K	X	Z	K
A	R	I	J	G	L	O	R	Y	K	R	E	R	D	E
I	L	O	F	G	H	J	O	Y	S	E	V	E	N	B
R	E	P	E	H	U	M	I	L	I	T	Y	I	O	E
U	P	P	L	K	J	H	T	R	E	F	D	F	G	R
X	R	A	E	R	T	H	G	F	D	A	V	T	W	O
Y	O	S	N	P	P	E	O	P	L	E	V	N	I	M
A	S	I	E	S	F	G	H	B	C	R	D	F	S	A
F	Y	D	E	C	N	A	R	E	V	E	S	R	E	P
N	M	I	S	U	T	E	M	L	E	H	Y	R	E	W

Puzzle 86

1. Who was Naomi's husband? (Ruth 1:1–2)

2. Who was Hannah's husband? (1 Samuel 1:1–2)

3. Which prophet did God tell to take a wife of harlotry? (Hosea 1:2)

4. Lapidoth was the husband of a _____ and _____ . (Judges 4:4–5)

5. Besides Aaron, who else made golden calves for Israel to worship? (1 Kings 12:25–29)

6. In the list of the Ten Commandments, what number is the commandment not to have graven images? (Exodus 20:4)

7. Hezekiah destroyed what brass, popular idol? (2 Kings 18:1, 4)

8. What idol of the Philistines fell facedown in front of the ark of the covenant? (1 Samuel 5:1–3)

9. Into what did King Josiah transform the places of idolatry? (2 Kings 23:13–14)

10. When Jacob was leaving Laban, which one of Jacob's family members stole Laban's idols? (Genesis 31:34)

11. Men were building a what when God confused their speech and language? (Genesis 11:4–9)

12. Some of the graven images people worshipped were made of _____ . (2 Chronicles 24:18 NKJV)

13. The only mention of an idol in the New Testament is the goddess Diana, whose shrine was in what city? (Acts 19:24–28)

14. What was the name of the silversmith who made shrines of Diana and started a riot to get rid of Paul? (Acts 19:24)

15. The worshippers of Diana thought her image fell down from _____ . (Acts 19:35 NKJV)

16. Fill in the blank: Jeremiah said that the people had become _____ with their idols. (Jeremiah 50:38 NKJV)

17. Zechariah said that idols speak what? (Zechariah 10:2 NKJV)

18. Who said, "Little children, keep yourselves from idols"? (1 John 5:21)

19. Fill in the blanks: Revelation 9:20 says that idols can neither _____ nor _____ nor _____ . (Revelation 9:20)

20. Romans 8:29 says we are to be conformed to the image of God's _____ .

```
A  F  D  S  E  N  O  I  S  U  L  E  D  R  T
M  S  U  I  O  P  A  T  O  W  E  R  P  E  T
D  U  F  S  R  A  E  H  W  E  H  T  R  W  H
V  S  E  I  R  E  T  E  M  E  C  F  O  G  G
E  E  R  T  Y  M  S  J  K  L  A  Y  P  L  O
A  H  N  O  G  A  D  E  R  Y  R  T  H  R  S
S  P  F  T  Y  O  E  R  E  U  I  O  E  H  U
U  E  Y  T  R  B  E  N  M  K  K  L  T  C  I
K  I  C  B  W  O  O  D  D  F  A  D  E  E  R
L  N  L  K  J  R  T  R  E  H  G  N  S  L  T
A  S  D  S  U  E  Z  W  E  R  A  X  S  E  E
W  A  O  B  N  J  U  D  G  E  Y  Z  E  M  M
A  N  S  F  R  T  H  J  S  K  L  O  P  I  E
U  E  Y  T  R  N  H  O  J  W  E  D  F  L  D
A  S  D  F  G  H  H  A  N  A  K  L  E  E  F
```

PUZZLE 87

1. Who said, "Man is the image and glory of God"? (1 Corinthians 11:7)
2. To whom was Jesus speaking when He said, "He who has seen Me has seen the Father"? (John 14:8–9 NKJV)
3. Fill in the blank: "Who, being in the form of God, did not consider it _____ to be equal with God." (Philippians 2:6 NKJV)
4. Fill in the blanks: Psalm 139:14 says, "I am _____ and _____ made."
5. Who said, "In Him we live and move and have our being?" (Acts 17:28 NKJV)
6. Jacob purchased Esau's birthright for a bowl of what? (Genesis 25:31, 34)
7. Jacob used skins of what to disguise himself as Esau? (Genesis 27:16)
8. Jacob was renamed _____ . (Genesis 32:27–28; 35:9–10)
9. Where can you find Esau's story in the Bible?
10. Who was Esau's mother? (Genesis 25:20–26)
11. Esau liked to what? (Genesis 25:27)
12. Esau planned to _____ Jacob after Jacob stole his birthright. (Genesis 27:41)
13. Esau married a descendant of whom? (Genesis 28:9)
14. Jacob called himself Esau's what? (Genesis 33:5)
15. Fill in the blank: "So Esau returned that day on his way unto _____ ." (Genesis 33:16)
16. God told Jeremiah that He had _____ him before he was born. (Jeremiah 1:5)
17. When the priests and prophets tried to kill Jeremiah, the _____ and the _____ saved him. (Jeremiah 26:16)
18. A _____ prophet was put to death because he spoke against Jeremiah and the Lord. (Jeremiah 28:11–17)
19. Where did the captains of the remnant of Judah take Jeremiah when the Babylonians conquered Israel? (Jeremiah 43:5–7)

20. Who was promised that he would not die until he saw the Messiah come? (Luke 2:25-26)

```
K R I P R I N C E S T H E Y U
T A S F D E S K O L F O P G J
P V R B Y L L U F R E D N O W
Y G A H D Z P X C D A S B A N
G O E U Y R E B B O R A S T R
E X L N F E B V N M F I G S H
Y S E T E V B P O L U A P S E
L A G J K S I U Y T L R E F D
E S W E R S I T F A L S E Y E
A T N A V R E S L K Y D S A N
M E A N O E M I S D F G U P I
H P E O P L E T R S D Z A K A
S L L I K E R T Y V H U J L D
I E R E D F S A P I L I H P R
Z A G J H A K E B E R W U Y O
```

PUZZLE 88

1. When someone called Jesus "good Master," Jesus said, "There is none good but. . . _____ ." (Mark 10:18)

2. Who was Caesar when Jesus was born? (Luke 2:1)

3. Jesus was in Jerusalem for the _____ of _____ when He got separated from His parents. (Luke 2:41)

4. How many days did Jesus' parents search before they found Him? (Luke 2:46)

5. Who are the five women mentioned in Jesus' genealogy in Matthew 1? (NIV)

6. Jesus talked about the end times from the Mount of what? (Matthew 24:3)

7. Did Jesus ever sing? (Matthew 26:30)

8. Fill in the blank: John said Jesus was full of grace and what? (John 1:14)

9. Fill in the blanks: Luke says the young boy Jesus grew in _____ , in _____ , in favor with _____ and _____ . (Luke 2:52)

10. In John 14:6, what three things did Jesus say He is?

11. When Satan tempted Jesus, he took Him to a mountain and what other place? (Matthew 4:1–11)

12. Complete the sentence: "I am _____ and _____ in heart." (Matthew 11:29)

13. When asked directly, "Whom say ye that I am?" Peter replied, "Thou are the _____ ." (Mark 8:29)

14. Complete Jesus' promise: "I am with you _____ and unto the _____ of the _____ ." (Matthew 28:20)

15. Fill in the blank: I am the light of the world: he that followeth me shall not walk in darkness, but shall have the light of _____ . (John 8:12)

16. Jesus said, "I am the _____ , and the life" while speaking to Martha about her brother Lazarus who had died. (John 11:23–25)

17. After saying, "I am the way, the truth, and the life," how many ways did Jesus list that a man could come to the Father? (John 14:6)

18. After saying, "I am the vine," Jesus described His Father as the what? (John 15:1)

19. Fill in the blank: Jesus said, "I am the vine, ye are the _____ ." (John 15:5)

20. When the cock crowed for the third time, Jesus looked at whom? (Luke 22:61)

A	T	Y	R	M	U	W	H	T	U	R	T	I	P	R
U	G	H	E	N	A	M	D	N	A	B	S	U	H	G
R	E	T	S	Y	Y	N	A	X	C	S	A	H	O	E
E	X	A	U	G	U	S	T	U	S	B	E	D	L	F
T	S	I	R	T	E	R	A	H	A	B	F	A	I	I
E	Y	N	R	O	N	E	M	B	R	Y	D	X	V	L
P	A	M	E	E	K	A	A	M	U	E	L	Y	E	A
A	W	L	C	K	R	D	R	C	T	N	E	W	S	B
A	L	W	T	Y	S	R	T	Y	H	S	U	D	N	E
P	A	L	I	F	E	U	Y	T	I	C	Y	L	O	H
R	E	V	O	S	S	A	P	E	R	U	T	A	T	S
A	S	D	N	T	D	Y	G	W	O	R	L	D	R	H
N	V	C	T	R	L	O	W	L	Y	U	H	J	U	T
A	D	E	S	T	D	E	M	C	H	R	I	S	T	A
O	P	S	E	H	C	N	A	R	B	X	C	V	H	B

Puzzle 89

1. Jesus told His apostles it was written that He would be reckoned among whom? (Luke 22:37)

2. What was the name of the garden where Jesus prayed? (Matthew 26:36)

3. When Jesus prayed in the garden, He asked that the hour might _____ from Him. (Mark 14:35)

4. Fill in the blank: The spirit indeed is willing, but the flesh is _____ . (Matthew 26:41)

5. How many times did Jesus pray the same words? (Matthew 26:44)

6. Jesus told those who came to arrest Him at night that "This is your _____ , and the power of _____ ." (Luke 22:53)

7. When Jesus stated that He was the one they sought, the men who came to arrest Him went _____ and fell to the _____ . (John 18:6)

8. Peter cut off which one of Malchus's ears? (John 18:10)

9. Fill in the blanks: Jesus told Peter, "Put up again thy _____ into his place: for all they that take the _____ shall perish with the _____ ." (Matthew 26:52)

10. How did Judas identify Jesus to the multitude that came to arrest Him? (Matthew 26:49)

11. How many pieces of silver did the chief priests and elders pay Judas to betray Jesus? (Matthew 27:3)

12. Fill in the blank: Judas said, "I have sinned in that I have betrayed the innocent _____ ." (Matthew 27:4)

13. Judas killed himself by what? (Matthew 27:5)

14. The chief priests bought the potter's field to bury whom? (Matthew 27:7)

15. In addition to Aceldama, the potter's field is also known as the field of what? (Matthew 27:8; Acts 1:19)

16. Pilate sent Jesus to Herod because Jesus was from where? (Luke 23:5, 7)

17. Fill in the blank: When Pilate asked if he should crucify their king, the chief priests said, "We have no king but _____ ." (John 19:15)

18. Whose wife said she had suffered many things in a dream because of Jesus? (Matthew 27:17, 19)

19. When the soldiers mocked Jesus, what did they put in His right hand? (Matthew 27:29)

20. The guards mocked Jesus by saying "Hail, _____ of the _____ !" (Mark 15:18)

```
T  Y  U  R  E  D  G  R  S  Y  T  R  I  H  T
R  A  S  E  A  C  D  G  R  O  U  N  D  E  E
S  A  D  C  X  H  E  G  O  U  I  O  T  N  B
E  R  O  T  Y  U  E  S  S  P  L  H  E  H  Y
V  Y  O  U  J  F  R  D  S  T  G  B  S  A  A
G  A  L  I  L  E  E  C  E  I  X  L  A  N  J
Z  S  B  A  C  K  W  A  R  D  K  O  N  G  V
A  R  R  T  Y  U  J  S  G  V  C  O  D  I  M
E  T  U  A  E  S  D  F  S  I  S  D  A  N  G
T  S  W  O  R  D  I  U  N  S  W  N  R  G  E
A  G  E  T  H  S  E  M  A  N  E  T  K  H  J
L  R  A  T  Y  U  M  P  R  C  B  E  N  R  T
I  X  K  I  N  G  D  F  T  H  R  E  E  G  H
P  Z  A  S  F  G  J  K  L  U  I  O  S  R  G
D  R  E  E  S  R  E  G  N  A  R  T  S  S  E
```

Puzzle 90

1. Who helped Jesus to carry His cross? (Matthew 27:32)
2. The sign Pilate put on Jesus' cross said "The King of the Jews" in how many languages? (Luke 23:38; John 19:19–20)
3. Fill in the blank: Although one man ran for vinegar, the others said, "Let be, let us see whether Elias [Elijah] will come to _____ him." (Matthew 27:49)
4. What kind of reed with a sponge soaked in vinegar was used to moisten Jesus' lips? (Mark 15:36; John 19:29)
5. What in the temple was torn from top to bottom when Jesus died? (Matthew 27:51)
6. Tombs were opened and saints came forth and marched to where as witnesses of Jesus' holiness? (Matthew 27:53)
7. Fill in the blank: The centurion said, " _____ this was the Son of God." (Matthew 27:54)
8. The centurion's statement about Jesus being the Son of God was made shortly after what event? (Matthew 27:54)
9. Some of the women who viewed the crucifixion from afar had followed Jesus from _____ and ministered to Him. (Mark 15:40–41)
10. Fill in the blank: "They shall look on him whom they _____ ." (John 19:37)
11. Jesus was buried by what two men? (John 19:38–42)
12. Joseph of where rolled the big stone across the tomb after Jesus' body had been placed in it? (Matthew 27:57–60)
13. Who rolled away the stone from Jesus' tomb? (Matthew 28:2)
14. Fill in the blanks: The two men in glowing clothes at the empty tomb asked the women, "Why do you look for the _____ among the _____ ?" (Luke 24:5)
15. What kind of clothes were left in the tomb? (John 20:6)

16. Did the disciples react with disbelief or rejoicing when Mary Magdalene and the other women told them Jesus was alive? (Luke 24:11)

17. The chief priests and elders gave what to the soldiers guarding the tomb when they found out it was empty? (Matthew 28:12)

18. Who said, "Unless I see the nail marks in his hands. . .I will not believe"? (John 20:24–25 NIV)

19. After Jesus arose, whom did He ask three times, "Do you love me?" (John 21:17)

20. Fill in the blank: Jesus said, "Therefore go and make disciples of all _____ , baptizing them in the name of the Father and of the Son and of the Holy Spirit." (Matthew 28:19 NIV)

```
A P D J R E T D F G H V O K F
T E R E A R T H Q U A K E S E
A T S R A Y U I R O P K A I I
X E N U M D U Y T E R V F M L
C R T S U Y M D N E E R S O E
A Y G A L I L E E R G H N N B
F L O L K M N C V E R T O Y S
S U L E T Y U R I O P M I N I
A R I M A T H E A R S D T A D
S T N G N I V I L E H R A Y U
A O E Q I U Y P W E Y A N L P
M O N E Y F G H J K S E Y E T
O O I U Y T R E W A S S D G F
H M N B B S U M E D O C I N O
T X E X T Y J O S E P H Z A P
```

Puzzle 91

1. Jesus was taken up into heaven in the vicinity of what small city? (Luke 24:50–51)

2. When Job was tested, how many children did he have? (Job 1:2)

3. Job was so concerned about _____ that he made sacrifices to the Lord on behalf of his sons, lest they _____ unintentionally. (Job 1:5)

4. Satan said that Job was only faithful because he had been so blessed and never been what? (Job 1:10–11)

5. The oxen and donkeys and all but one servant tending them were slaughtered by whom? (Job 1:15)

6. The sheep and all but one of the servants tending them were destroyed by what falling from heaven? (Job 1:16)

7. The camels and all but one servant were killed by whom? (Job 1:17)

8. Job's children were killed by what? (Job 1:18–19)

9. What did Job shave when he found out about his losses? (Job 1:20)

10. Fill in the blanks: Job said, " _____ came I out of my mother's womb, and _____ shall I return thither: the LORD gave, and the LORD hath taken away: blessed by the name of the LORD." (Job 1:21)

11. When Satan placed boils on him, Job scratched them with broken what? (Job 2:8)

12. How many friends arrived to comfort Job? (Job 2:11)

13. What were the names of Job's friends that visited? (Job 2:11)

14. Job's friends didn't speak to him for _____ days and _____ nights. (Job 2:13)

15. The Lord told Job's visitors that He was what at them? (Job 42:7)

16. Fill in the blank: Isaiah wrote, "A voice of one calling: 'in the _____ prepare the way for the LORD.'" (Isaiah 40:3 NIV)

17. What was the name of the angel who announced John the Baptist's birth to his father? (Luke 1:19)

18. Because of his unbelief, what condition struck John's father until the time his son, John the Baptist, was named? (Luke 1:13, 20)
19. Who were the parents of John the Baptist? (Luke 1:5, 13)
20. Fill in the blank: "He shall go before him in the spirit and power of Elias [Elijah]. . .to make ready a people _____ for the Lord. (Luke 1:17)

M	N	P	S	A	I	R	A	H	C	A	Z	E	T	H
X	W	E	L	Y	K	G	T	S	E	F	V	F	H	N
A	G	A	B	R	I	E	L	Y	U	I	H	E	A	D
S	T	U	N	G	F	G	B	N	M	R	U	I	O	P
S	E	V	E	N	E	R	T	Y	D	E	T	S	E	T
E	P	E	U	A	P	I	S	N	A	E	B	A	S	J
N	R	A	H	P	O	Z	N	N	Y	U	E	N	S	T
E	E	E	R	H	T	M	A	Y	N	A	H	T	E	B
T	P	L	T	R	T	K	E	E	V	M	I	U	N	T
U	A	I	A	W	E	T	D	N	I	W	Y	U	R	I
M	R	P	O	D	R	F	L	T	Y	N	E	V	E	S
R	E	H	T	G	Y	N	A	K	E	D	E	A	D	S
E	D	A	N	M	P	O	H	I	J	H	T	Y	L	S
A	S	Z	D	E	W	Q	C	U	D	A	D	L	I	B
Y	C	H	T	E	B	A	S	I	L	E	I	N	W	B

Puzzle 92

1. John's father told others of his newborn son's name by writing it on what? (Luke 1:63 NIV)

2. Who was the Caesar when John the Baptist began preaching? (Luke 3:1–3)

3. Fill in the blank: John the Baptist told soldiers, "Don't extort money and don't accuse people falsely—be content with your _____ ." (Luke 3:14 NIV)

4. Fill in the blanks: John said he baptized with water, but the one who came after would baptize with the _____ _____ . (Mark 1:8 NIV)

5. According to the Gospel of John, what expression did John the Baptist use to describe Jesus? (John 1:29)

6. In speaking of Jesus, what did John say he was unworthy to _____ the _____ of Jesus. (Mark 1:7)

7. John the Baptist described the Pharisees and Sadducees as a brood of what? (Matthew 3:7)

8. Herod the tetrarch believed that _____ was John the Baptist raised from the dead. (Matthew 14:1–2)

9. What was the name of the woman who John the Baptist said was not lawful for Herod to have? (Matthew 14:3–4)

10. God asked Jonah to go where? (Jonah 1:1–2)

11. Jonah boarded a ship to Tarshish because he wanted to _____ from the Lord. (Jonah 1:3)

12. God caused what to happen to the sea after Jonah boarded the ship? (Jonah 1:4)

13. The Bible says Jonah was swallowed by a _____ . (Jonah 1:17)

14. Fill in the blank: But I will sacrifice unto thee with the voice of thanksgiving; I will pay that that I have vowed. _____ is of the LORD. (Jonah 2:9)

15. Jonah told the Ninevites that they had how many days left before God would destroy them? (Jonah 3:4)

16. After the Ninevites heard the message from God delivered by Jonah, they _____ and wore _____ . (Jonah 3:5)

17. The plant that shaded Jonah as he waited to see what would happen to the city was a what? (Jonah 4:6)

18. The plant was destroyed by a what? (Jonah 4:7)

19. The Lord raised up _____ to deliver the Israelites from their enemies. (Judges 2:16)

20. Othniel, the first judge of Israel, was the son of Joshua's brother or Caleb's brother? (Judges 3:9)

A	R	E	T	Y	I	Y	D	F	G	H	J	K	M	O
G	C	A	L	E	B	T	X	F	G	M	R	O	W	L
O	A	X	S	F	I	R	O	J	R	T	S	Y	N	M
U	Z	S	A	I	D	O	R	E	H	E	H	U	R	T
R	M	N	E	S	T	F	E	S	M	R	O	T	S	Y
D	C	X	Y	H	R	B	S	U	I	R	E	B	I	T
A	W	T	Y	D	O	V	U	S	I	P	S	E	N	L
E	D	N	M	O	T	I	R	I	P	S	Y	L	O	H
R	E	T	C	G	U	P	W	E	R	T	C	O	I	B
W	T	N	B	F	L	E	E	T	I	U	S	Q	T	A
A	S	E	W	O	U	R	I	P	T	E	L	B	A	T
X	A	I	V	B	D	S	E	G	D	U	J	A	V	Y
S	F	E	R	M	Y	U	I	O	P	K	L	B	L	A
E	T	Y	H	A	H	E	V	E	N	I	N	E	A	P
S	D	R	I	L	H	T	O	L	C	K	C	A	S	W

Puzzle 93

1. Ehud went against Eglon, the king of Moab or Edom? (Judges 3:15)

2. Who campaigned to make himself a judge? (Judges 9:1–2)

3. Abimelech was the son of _____ , also known as Jerub-baal. (Judges 6:32, 9:1 NIV)

4. Was Ibzan from Bethlehem or Jerusalem? (Judges 12:8)

5. Abdon had how many sons? (Judges 12:13–14)

6. Fill in the blank: After each judge died, the children of Israel did _____ in the sight of the Lord. (Judges 13:1)

7. Jabin was the king of what place? (Judges 4:2)

8. Who was the captain of Jabin's army? (Judges 4:2)

9. Fill in the blanks: Deborah dwelt under a _____ _____. (Judges 4:5)

10. Who told Deborah he would go fight only if she went with him? (Judges 4:8)

11. Fill in the blank: Deborah told Barak that the Lord would sell Sisera into the hand of a _____ . (Judges 4:9)

12. Heber was a Kenite or a Moabite? (Judges 4:11)

13. Sisera fled to the tent of Heber and Heber's wife, _____ , because there was peace between Jabin and Heber. (Judges 4:17)

14. What did Jael give Sisera to drink when he came to her tent? (Judges 4:18–19)

15. What two people said "Praise ye the LORD for the avenging of Israel"? (Judges 5:1–2)

16. Fill in the blanks: The kingdom of God is like a man who sowed _____ _____ in his field. (Matthew 13:24–30)

17. Fill in the blank: The kingdom of God is like a _____ seed. (Matthew 13:31–32)

18. Fill in the blank: The kingdom of God is like a _____ hidden in a field. (Matthew 13:44)

19. The kingdom of God is like a merchant seeking beautiful what? (Matthew 13:45-46)

20. Who was the first king of Israel? (1 Samuel 9:1-2, 15-16)

```
E S G H J R A S T K A R A B Y
N M H S A U L I B L U R G H J
A S C H Y E R A X V E J H E S
U D E E S D O O G S T A H G L
O P L R E M T Y I U J K J C R
W T E Y K R E S D D F M N B A
E Q M V L F G K E K A R A B E
R F I V I Y T R O F T E D V P
U N B E M L R T N Y X E Z E I
S N A A N A C E R T Y R P T O
A B E T H L E H E M Y T X I M
E K J T R E M N B W O M A N E
R D R A T S U M A E R L Y E V
T X C V B N D E B O R A H K A
E W E R T Y U I O M N P Y S E
```

Puzzle 94

1. How many days was the shortest reign of a king of Israel? (1 Kings 16:15)

2. After the kingdom split into the ten northern tribes (Israel) and the two southern tribes (Judah), who was the first king of the northern tribes? (1 Kings 11:31)

3. After the kingdom split, how many kings did the ten northern tribes have before they were taken into captivity? (1 Kings 12:20– 2 Kings 17)

4. What nation took the ten northern tribes into captivity? (2 Kings 17:6)

5. Who was king when the ten northern tribes were taken into captivity? (2 Kings 17:6)

6. After the kingdom split, how many years was the longest reign of a king over Israel? (2 Kings 14:23)

7. What son of a king of Judah married the daughter of a king of Israel? (2 Chronicles 21:1, 6)

8. What wicked king and queen killed Naboth so they could steal his vineyard? (1 Kings 21)

9. What king drove his chariot furiously? (2 Kings 9:20)

10. Who does the Bible say did evil in the sight of the Lord more than all who were before him? (1 Kings 16:30)

11. What ruler followed Joash as king of Israel? (2 Kings 13:13)

12. What king got a withered hand because he tried to have a prophet arrested? (1 Kings 13:4)

13. Who was king of Israel for only seven days? (1 Kings 16:15)

14. Omri became king of Israel because _____ , his rival, died. (1 Kings 16:22)

15. What king of Israel reigned at the same time as a king of Judah with the same name? (2 Kings 13:10–11; 2 Kings 12:2)

16. Who was the first king of Judah? (1 Samuel 10:21–24)

17. What king's grandmother tried to kill all of her grandchildren so she could be queen? (2 Chronicles 22:10–11)

18. Like, Ahab, which king built up a grove for the worship of false gods? (2 Kings 21:1–3)

19. How many times was David anointed king? (1 Samuel 16:13; 2 Samuel 2:4; 5:3)

20. What prophet, along with Zadok the priest, anointed Solomon king? (1 Kings 1:34)

```
W E R L L E B E Z E J A T Y U
M K I Y U T R E F N G J K B J
A D F N B A Y E I O C U A M P
Z J X W E Y S T R Y R H E K L
S E T I B N I A M T A T H Y B
T H E R F G H A I R Y S S A S
X O R T A H J I Z O T M O N L
M A O B O R E J T F N U H E J
T S Y H H G R S E V E N T N E
D H I P S L O A S Z W J K M R
A G F D H A B J K A T L E Y O
V N M M A R O H E J N D F V B
E D E B A H A J R T Y A K I O
N A H T A N M T H R E E M L A
T C V E S A Y T R E V B N M M
```

Puzzle 95

1. Who was the king when the kingdom split into the ten northern tribes (Israel) and the two southern tribes (Judah)? (1 Kings 12:19–21)

2. About what boy king does the Bible say there was none before him or after him "that turned to the LORD with all his heart"? (2 Kings 23:24–25)

3. Uzziah was one of the really good kings of Judah, but God struck him with leprosy because he burned _____ in the temple. (2 Chronicles 26:19–20)

4. What king had a brother named Adonijah who tried to steal his throne? (1 Kings 1:5, 17–18)

5. Who was king when the kingdom of Judah was taken into Babylonian captivity? (2 Chronicles 36:5–6)

6. God gave Solomon riches, wealth, and honor because he asked for what? (2 Chronicles 1:11–12)

7. Who was the youngest king of Judah? (2 Kings 11)

8. When the golden shields Solomon had made for the temple were stolen, King Rehoboam replaced them with shields made of what? (1 Kings 14:27)

9. What king was responsible for bringing a guaranteed water supply to Jerusalem? (2 Kings 20:20; 2 Chronicles 32:30)

10. What youngest son of Jehoram was made king of Judah because all of his brothers were killed? (2 Chronicles 22:1)

11. What king of Judah cleared the temple of objects used to worship Baal? (2 Kings 23:4, 16)

12. What king of Judah was blinded by his captors? (Jeremiah 39:7)

13. Whose reign of fifty-five years was the longest of the kings of Judah? (2 Kings 21:1)

14. Which king of Egypt took away the treasure of Jerusalem during the reign of Rehoboam? (1 Kings 14:25–26)

15. How many kings did the United Kingdom of Israel have before it split into the northern and southern kingdoms? (1 Samuel 10:21-24; 2 Samuel 5:2-3; 1 Kings 4:1; 1 Kings 12:1)

16. Who were the four kings? (1 Samuel 10:21-24; 2 Samuel 5:2-3; 1 Kings 4:1; 1 Kings 12:1)

17. When God was giving Moses instructions concerning the king, who did God say was to choose the king? (Deuteronomy 17:15)

18. God told Moses that the king was not to multiply horses, wives, _____ , and _____ . (Deuteronomy 17:16-17)

19. A king was supposed to write a copy of the what when he became king? (Deuteronomy 17:18)

20. Whose feelings were hurt because Israel wanted a king? (1 Samuel 8:6-7)

```
X  V  B  N  A  M  A  O  B  O  H  E  R  T  Y
A  Z  E  D  E  K  I  A  H  M  K  L  E  H  J
S  G  F  S  R  T  M  U  O  P  R  R  Z  E  V
L  Y  M  O  D  S  I  W  A  N  M  U  N  I  B
E  X  A  L  K  I  K  D  A  V  I  D  O  E  R
U  Z  N  O  A  M  A  O  B  O  H  E  R  F  Y
M  D  A  M  H  R  I  T  W  E  J  N  B  H  H
A  L  S  O  S  N  O  M  O  L  O  S  N  N  A
S  G  S  N  I  R  H  T  Y  Z  A  E  V  A  I
N  O  E  G  H  D  E  L  U  A  S  C  X  O  S
M  D  H  D  S  R  J  Y  T  F  H  N  A  B  O
D  F  L  K  A  H  S  H  S  H  A  I  S  O  J
N  O  B  H  A  I  Z  A  H  A  G  T  H  H  E
G  E  W  A  L  T  Y  H  A  I  K  E  Z  E  H
P  E  X  D  C  V  B  N  S  I  L  V  E  R  S
```

Puzzle 96

1. What king solicited the services of the witch of Endor? (1 Samuel 28:7–25)

2. What king of Israel notably had three hundred concubines? (1 Kings 11:3)

3. What king's wife despised him for dancing before the Lord? (2 Samuel 6:16)

4. King Saul fell on what and died? (1 Samuel 31:4)

5. How many years was David king of Judah before he also became king of Israel? (2 Samuel 5:5)

6. When David was made king of Judah, who was made king of Israel? (2 Samuel 2:10)

7. Balak, who hired Balaam to curse the Israelites, was king of what nation? (Numbers 22:1–6)

8. King Hiram (or Huram), from whom Solomon got materials to build the temple, was king of what country? (2 Chronicles 2:3)

9. Melchizedek was a priest, but he was also king of? (Genesis 14:18)

10. Nebuchadnezzar took which kingdom captive, Judah or Israel? (2 Chronicles 36:5–6)

11. The king of what country took the northern kingdom of Israel captive? (2 Kings 17:6)

12. Which king allowed the Israelites to return to Jerusalem from their captivity in Babylon? (Ezra 1:1–2)

13. Which king saw the handwriting on the wall? (Daniel 5:1–5)

14. Who saved a king's life after he overheard two eunuchs plotting against the king? (Esther 2:21–23)

15. What king threw Daniel into the lions' den? (Daniel 5:31; 6:16–23)

16. What king did Saul refuse to kill in direct disobedience to God's command? (1 Samuel 15:8–9)

17. Whom did King Xerxes ask, "What should be done for the man the king delights to honor?" (Esther 6:6 NIV)

18. What name applies to a line of wicked kings from the time of Jesus through the apostle Paul? (Matthew 2:1-20; Mark 8:15; Acts 12; Acts 25)

19. The Feast of Tabernacles and the Feast of Booths lasted how many days each? (Leviticus 23:41-43)

20. Who will judge the angels? (1 Corinthians 6:3)

```
A  G  H  J  R  T  E  R  Y  U  I  O  K  L  P
Y  S  E  F  D  S  H  I  A  C  E  D  R  O  M
S  D  T  M  E  L  A  S  N  R  M  E  R  T  J
D  O  R  E  H  I  D  E  Y  B  N  E  V  E  S
S  A  E  H  G  J  U  T  N  I  O  P  D  E  R
O  L  S  K  M  A  J  I  N  E  B  Y  R  H  T
X  D  F  U  V  I  G  B  Z  E  V  T  O  T  Y
R  N  E  A  R  R  K  A  M  N  G  E  W  E  H
T  A  H  F  J  Y  N  O  M  O  L  O  S  H  L
X  M  T  R  E  S  C  M  D  F  U  G  H  S  P
C  A  A  E  R  S  G  D  H  E  A  W  Q  O  U
C  H  N  M  R  A  Z  Z  A  H  S  L  E  B  L
A  S  D  F  E  R  T  Y  H  V  J  K  I  H  P
A  S  E  S  D  C  V  D  A  R  I  U  S  S  E
S  N  A  I  T  S  I  R  H  C  O  D  E  I  R
```

PUZZLE 97

1. Who spoke of an angel who had redeemed him from evil? (Genesis 48:14, 16)

2. What were the Israelites compelled to do for Pharaoh? (Exodus 1:11)

3. Which church was told they are alive but dead? (Revelation 3:1)

4. Which church was told it had left its first love? (Revelation 2:1, 4)

5. Fill in the blanks: God says in the new covenant He will be their _____ and they shall be His _____ . (Jeremiah 31:33)

6. Who said, "Increase our faith"? (Luke 17:5)

7. Who was Peter and Andrew's father? (Matthew 16:17)

8. Who was the father of John the Baptist? (Luke 1:59)

9. Who was the father of James and John? (Matthew 4:21)

10. When told that his sons had been killed in battle and the ark of the covenant had been taken, what father fell over backward and died of a broken neck? (1 Samuel 4:16–18)

11. Who was Abram's father? (Genesis 11:31)

12. Who was the father of Shem, Ham, and Japheth? (Genesis 5:32)

13. When Abraham died, what cave did his sons bury him in? (Genesis 25:9–10)

14. Noah offered one of every clean _____ and _____ on the altar he built when he came out of the ark. (Genesis 8:20)

15. Souls of the _____ were under the altar in heaven. (Revelation 6:9)

16. The Pharisees said the most binding oath was one sworn by the _____ that was on the altar. (Matthew 23:18)

17. An angel of the Lord told Paul that the ship he was on would _____ _____ while they were in the midst of a bad storm. (Acts 27:26 NIV)

18. To whose father did the angel of the Lord appear and then ascend to heaven in the flame from the altar? (Judges 13:19–29)

19. In Hebrews 13:2, we are told to practice hospitality because we might be entertaining _____ unawares.
20. In Revelation 5:11 and 7:11, the angels in heaven are standing around the _____ .

```
D N U O R G A B V S E U I D X
M A C H P E L A H O H G F S A
N E S Y U W I S P L K B L A E
C X A N I M A L H F D E G T Y
D R I B T E R A H W G N R T E
A F R N H T F I G N M O I Z P
N O A H E J K N A O L R P O H
A F H R A G H Q U S S H I L E
X H C U P E R T I M U T L K S
U H A N O J I F V A E N B J U
F D Z A S E R T M S I D R A S
Y R E M T N K L P O I Y D C U
X S W Q L U E E D E B E Z O X
T G H S E I T I C D L I U B G
C V B A S Y E L P O E P O L T
```

Puzzle 98

1. The angels have charge over the righteous to bear you up in their hands and take you to _____ . (Psalm 91:11–12)

2. In David's time, God sent an angel to Jerusalem to _____ the city. (1 Chronicles 21:15)

3. An angel appeared to Zechariah the prophet to answer his questions and interpret his _____ . (Zechariah 4:4–7, 12–14; 5:1–3)

4. The angels in heaven spend their time worshipping the Lamb who was _____ . (Revelation 5:11–12)

5. In Revelation 10:6, an angel declared that there should be _____ no longer.

6. According to Acts 10:9–12, Peter saw animals, reptiles, and _____ in a sheet, coming down from heaven by its four corners.

7. Paul was referring to evil workers who insisted on _____ for Gentiles when he warned the Philippians to "beware of dogs" in Philippians 3:2.

8. According to Exodus 30:26–27, the ark of the covenant, the table of _____ , lampstand, and incense altar were all anointed.

9. According to Matthew 19:28, who will judge the tribes of Israel in the future?

10. Peter was sent to preach to _____ , who was a Gentile, devout man, and a centurion. (Acts 10:1–2)

11. Jesus said that what happened to the prophets would happen to the apostles, some would be killed, some would be _____ . (Luke 11:49)

12. The members of the church continued in the apostles' _____ and _____ . (Acts 2:42)

13. The early Christians lay all the _____ things they wanted to share at the apostles' feet. (Acts 4:34–35)

14. According to 1 Corinthians 1:1, Paul became an apostle because he was _____ .

15. The rings for the poles of the ark of the covenant were attached on its four _____ . (Exodus 25:12 NIV)

16. Who inspected the ark of the covenant after it was built? (Exodus 39:43)

17. While the ark was being moved, who died because the oxen pulling the cart stumbled and he touched the ark in an attempt to right it? (2 Samuel 6:6)

18. "Blessed be those who bless you" was part of the blessing that Isaac gave _____ . (Genesis 27:29-30 NKJV)

19. The king of Moab was angry at Balaam because Balaam _____ the Israelites instead of _____ . (Numbers 24:13 NKJV)

C	E	R	T	G	N	I	S	R	U	C	Y	U	P	L
A	X	N	Y	E	N	B	V	S	C	B	O	C	A	J
L	T	I	M	E	Z	T	Y	A	N	K	L	U	N	D
L	C	A	P	S	U	Z	Z	A	H	O	H	G	O	F
E	S	L	E	D	R	T	Y	A	S	C	I	X	I	H
D	E	S	T	R	O	Y	M	N	K	E	L	S	S	P
A	L	G	E	I	F	W	E	R	H	J	S	K	I	L
Q	T	A	R	B	S	D	M	N	V	B	X	O	C	V
U	S	B	L	E	S	S	E	D	T	Z	Z	U	M	E
D	O	C	T	R	I	N	E	N	E	J	K	Z	U	N
C	P	E	R	S	E	C	U	T	E	D	N	M	C	E
M	A	T	E	R	I	A	L	E	F	R	T	Y	R	V
F	E	L	L	O	W	S	H	I	P	S	D	F	I	A
Y	H	O	P	C	S	U	I	L	E	N	R	O	C	E
A	T	S	D	F	D	A	E	R	B	W	O	H	S	H

Puzzle 99

1. Children of the _____ woman rise up and call her blessed. (Proverbs 31:10, 28)

2. The Lord says that we must bring all of our _____ into His storehouse and He will pour out such blessing upon us that we won't have room to receive it. (Malachi 3:10)

3. Whom did God say He had called in righteousness to open blind eyes? (Isaiah 42:1, 6-7)

4. Paul said the _____ of this age had blinded the perishing to the gospel. (2 Corinthians 4:4)

5. The only time that Isaac and Ishmael cooperated with each other is when they _____ their father, Abraham. (Genesis 25:8-9)

6. What were the names of Abram's two brothers? (Genesis 11:27)

7. On the first trip to Egypt, Joseph accused his brothers of being _____ to frighten them into telling him more about his father and the family. (Genesis 42:9)

8. According to 2 Kings 17:26, the people the king of Assyria sent to Samaria were killed by what?

9. Pharaoh was afraid that Israel would join Egypt's _____ and fight against Egypt. (Exodus 1:10)

10. To subdue the Israelites, Pharaoh first set _____ over them. (Exodus 1:11)

11. The more the Israelites were afflicted, the more they _____ . (Exodus 1:12)

12. These children all had their birth divinely announced: Ishmael, Isaac, _____ , John the Baptist, and Jesus. (Judges 13:5)

13. The Lord intervened on behalf of Leah and Rachel so they could _____ . (Genesis 29:31; 30:22)

14. Who was the first church written to? (Revelation 2-3)

15. Barnabas was a part of which church? (Acts 13:1)

16. Who was an elder who sat in the gate of Sodom? (Genesis 19:1)

17. Who told Pharaoh that the Hebrew women gave birth before they got there? (Exodus 1:19)

18. Joshua told his army that if they had _____ , the Lord would fight for them. (Joshua 10:25)

19. When David instructed Solomon to build the _____ , he told him to be of good courage. (1 Chronicles 22:6–14)

20. According to Exodus 19:5, the covenant God made with the Israelites through Moses was _____ .

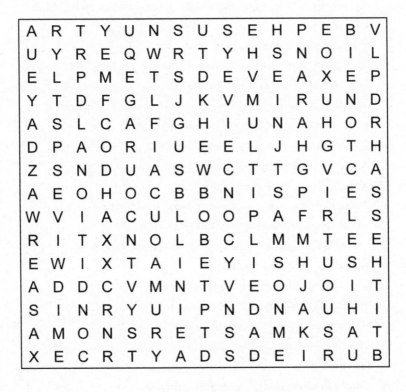

```
A R T Y U N S U S E H P E B V
U Y R E Q W R T Y H S N O I L
E L P M E T S D E V E A X E P
Y T D F G L J K V M I R U N D
A S L C A F G H I U N A H O R
D P A O R I U E E L J H G T H
Z S N D U A S W C T T G V C A
A E O H O C B B N I S P I E S
W V I A C U L O O P A F R L S
R I T X N O L B C L M M T E E
E W I X T A I E Y I S H U S H
A D D C V M N T V E O J O I T
S I N R Y U I P N D N A U H I
A M O N S R E T S A M K S A T
X E C R T Y A D S D E I R U B
```

Puzzle 100

1. According to Genesis 1:20, God called for sea creatures before he spoke _____ into existence.

2. According to Genesis 1:3–2:3, this is the order of creation: Light, skies and seas, land and plants and flowers and trees, sun and moon and stars, birds and fish, animals and man, _____ .

3. According to Deuteronomy 27:12–13, God designated a mountain of _____ and a mountain of _____ .

4. According to Deuteronomy 21:22–23, a man hanged on a _____ is cursed.

5. Whose Babylonian name was Belteshazzar? (Daniel 1:7)

6. According to Daniel 6:5, the men knew they couldn't find any fault against Daniel unless it had to do with the _____ of Daniel's God.

7. Who was tricked into passing a law stating that no one could ask a petition of anyone but him for thirty days? (Daniel 6:7)

8. Daniel was a prince of _____ before he was taken to Babylon.

9. According to Numbers 27:7, if a Hebrew man had no sons, his _____ could inherit his land.

10. Jesus' hair was _____ as snow and wool. (Revelation 1:14)

11. Jesus' feet were like what metal? (Revelation 1:15)

12. When Jesus cleansed the temple, there were people selling _____ . (Matthew 21:12)

13. Who rebuked Joseph because he dreamed that the sun, moon, and eleven stars bowed down to him? (Genesis 37:7)

14. How many dreams did Joseph have? (Genesis 37:5–11)

15. Where were Joseph, the butler, and the bakers when Joseph interpreted their dreams? (Genesis 40:1–3)

16. Whose dream had a good interpretation—the baker's or the butler's? (Genesis 40:13)

17. Whose dream did Joseph interpret first, the baker's or the butler's? (Genesis 40:9–12)

18. Which dream did Pharaoh have first—the cows or the grain? (Genesis 41:2)

19. Who caused God to make the earth open up and swallow him because he spoke against Moses and Aaron and rejected the Lord? (Numbers 16:3, 30)

20. The earthquake that occurred when Jesus was on the cross caused what to open? (Matthew 27:52)

```
Y  U  I  O  S  D  E  W  R  T  K  L  X  D  A
J  H  S  E  V  A  R  G  D  S  J  A  C  O  B
A  K  S  G  H  J  K  H  A  D  U  J  W  V  T
S  O  C  X  N  B  V  N  M  A  I  T  U  E  Y
A  R  G  H  J  K  P  E  E  R  T  L  B  S  E
O  A  E  L  K  J  H  T  G  I  F  S  L  A  W
P  H  E  L  T  J  A  I  L  U  W  E  E  C  B
C  B  M  K  T  L  U  H  I  S  Y  T  S  R  E
A  S  D  F  E  U  R  W  W  T  Y  U  S  E  K
X  T  R  F  Y  U  B  P  O  B  N  M  I  T  L
A  S  D  F  S  R  E  L  T  U  B  E  N  H  G
B  I  A  W  E  S  K  J  T  R  E  H  G  G  J
C  F  O  X  V  Q  A  U  G  N  I  S  R  U  C
U  C  M  N  X  C  V  R  X  L  E  I  N  A  D
A  S  D  F  G  T  Y  U  B  I  B  I  R  D  S
```

Puzzle 101

1. Both Elijah and Elisha parted the _____ River. (2 Kings 2:8, 14)

2. Who cured the waters of Jericho with salt? (2 Kings 2:21–22)

3. According to 1 Kings 17:6, which prophet was kept alive by birds?

4. Elisha cured whose leprosy? (2 Kings 5:10, 14)

5. The ephod was to be made of the colors gold, blue, purple, and what? (Exodus 28:6)

6. Who did Adam blame for making him eat the forbidden fruit? (Genesis 3:12)

7. Aaron made the golden calf out of the Israelite's gold what? (Exodus 32:2–3)

8. According to Numbers 13:33, the spies who investigated Jordan said it couldn't be taken because of what?

9. The false gods of the Greeks, _____ , and Zeus, are mentioned in the Bible. (Acts 14:12 NIV)

10. The people of Babylon worshipped Succoth _____ . (2 Kings 17:28–31)

11. The people of Cuth worshipped _____ . (2 Kings 17:28–31)

12. The people of Hamath worshipped _____ . (2 Kings 17:28–31)

13. The gods Nibhaz and Tartak were worshipped by the _____ . (2 Kings 17:28–31)

14. The god Adrammelech was worshipped by the _____ . (2 Kings 17:28–31)

15. Ashtoreth was worshipped by the _____ . (1 Kings 11:5 NKJV)

16. The Moabites worshipped _____ . (1 Kings 11:7)

17. The Philistines worshipped _____ . (1 Samuel 5:2)

18. A seven-year famine occurred during the time of what prophet? (2 Kings 8:1–2)

19. What king humbled himself before the Lord and fasted? (1 Kings 21:26–27)

20. Who was afraid to build the temple? (1 Chronicles 22:11, 13)

```
O  N  T  R  B  E  S  N  A  I  N  O  D  I  S
H  O  G  N  E  R  G  A  L  S  A  L  K  J  H
E  G  I  A  N  T  S  W  T  Y  U  Q  I  O  P
H  A  C  N  O  V  B  T  E  L  R  A  C  S  E
S  D  E  D  T  T  Y  U  I  G  H  J  K  E  E
O  T  R  S  H  B  D  A  N  M  K  L  V  T  A
M  W  E  H  A  E  L  I  S  H  A  E  C  I  R
E  S  D  H  B  V  S  N  A  M  A  A  N  V  R
H  N  A  X  D  F  E  R  E  T  Y  U  I  R  I
C  O  M  E  A  R  B  N  L  J  O  R  D  A  N
A  M  I  Z  V  D  F  G  I  E  R  T  Y  H  G
S  O  H  U  I  O  T  Y  J  I  L  K  J  P  S
D  L  S  F  T  E  S  Z  A  H  S  I  L  E  E
I  O  A  S  E  M  R  E  H  C  V  B  A  S  Z
Z  S  M  E  S  O  T  R  I  B  V  S  D  F  G
```

ANSWER KEY

Puzzle 1

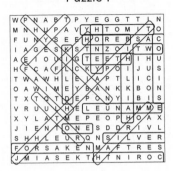

Puzzle 2

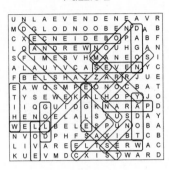

Puzzle 3

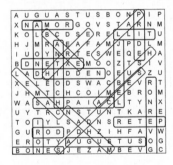

Puzzle 4

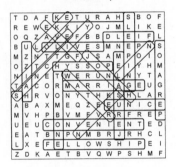

Puzzle 5

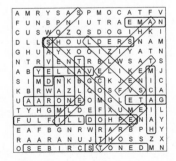

Puzzle 6

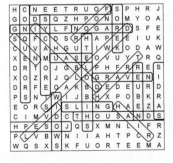

Puzzle 7

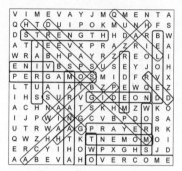

Puzzle 8

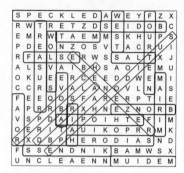

Puzzle 9

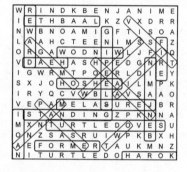

Puzzle 10

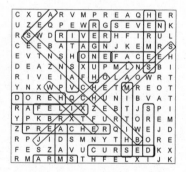

Puzzle 11

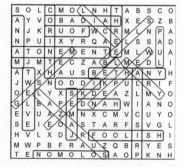

Puzzle 12

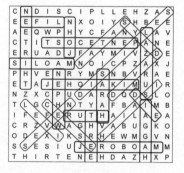

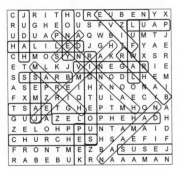

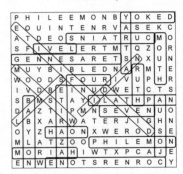

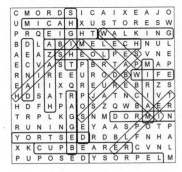

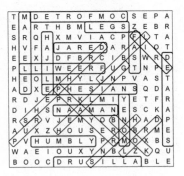

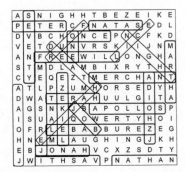

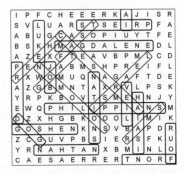

Puzzle 19

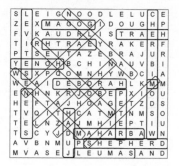

Puzzle 20

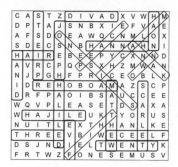

Puzzle 21

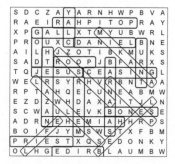

Puzzle 22

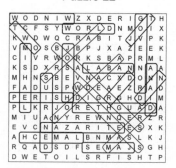

Puzzle 23

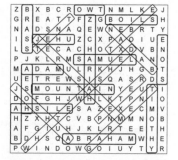

Puzzle 24

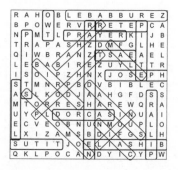

Puzzle 25

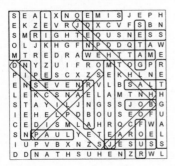

Puzzle 26

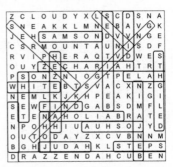

Puzzle 27

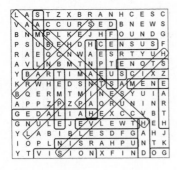

Puzzle 28

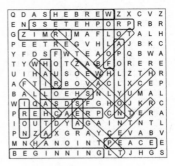

Puzzle 29

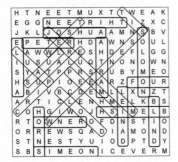

Puzzle 30

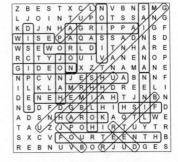

Puzzle 31

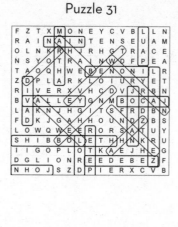

Puzzle 32

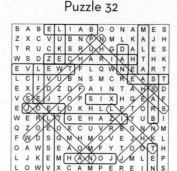

Puzzle 33

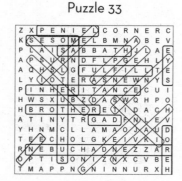

Puzzle 34

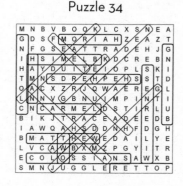

Puzzle 35

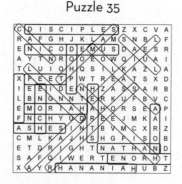

Puzzle 36

Puzzle 37

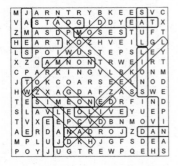

Puzzle 38

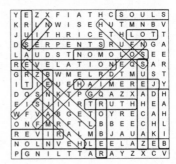

Puzzle 39

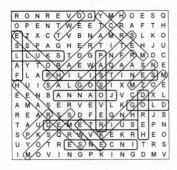

Puzzle 40

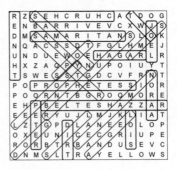

Puzzle 41

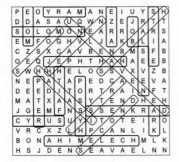

Puzzle 42

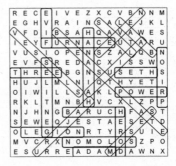

Puzzle 43

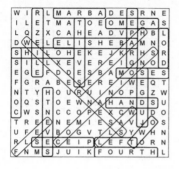

Puzzle 44

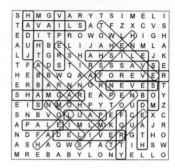

Puzzle 45

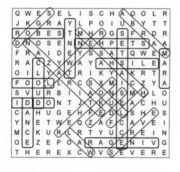

Puzzle 46

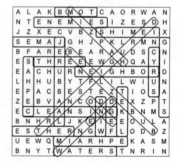

Puzzle 47

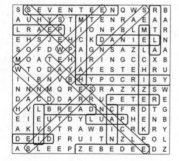

Puzzle 48

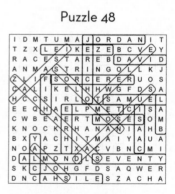

Puzzle 49

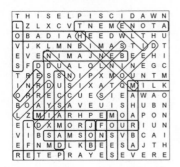

Puzzle 50

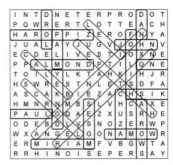

Puzzle 51

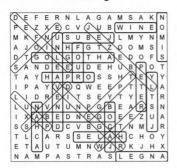

Puzzle 52

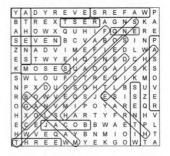

Puzzle 53

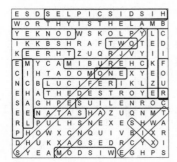

Puzzle 54

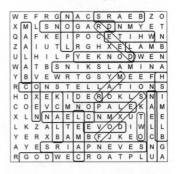

Puzzle 55

```
A D U S H I J A P E W A Q M X
P I L I H P M I H G I D E O N
N E X N J O C K L O P Z E S S
H D N A U Q W E I M N A V T D
O X Y I F H S T N E V A E H O
J Y T E N X S A F R E C O R
W E R Y T B V A N W A J K L E
C A H A J I L E J U C I V Y M
H K W A R C A L L E D M O P E
D I H A I M E H E N S D U L N
A B A R N A B A S X Y R P A E
B U T E A H P E T E R O D C D
Y N O M O L O S C Q U G L E L
A L T R E X K R A M N H O J O
M E I E C I M N E D L O G A G
```

Puzzle 56

```
E T U C E S R E P E L T Y A S
R A U H G K D R A W E R S H S
L Y O S R E K A M E C A E P E
A L J G E A R E L I V E R O N
X E B U A L I M K Y E H S A S
U S I H T A Z F C O I N W T U
A L F P J D E R A B N I S U O
L A I E D O E T Y L K E N M E
U F L S U M I T A T S R I H T
F O L I G D A K R E L U A S H
I K E E M O A W L O V P T E G
C I D W O L I O V N F U N X I
R E G N U H F S W U I M U P R
E Z T I R I P S N I R O O P E
M U Q S N E W M N B E L M C A
```

Puzzle 57

```
A G H E D R I H T Y T N E W T
N O I T A L E V E R J U D E G
Z D A R Z E E D C V O K M N O
A S D T R U U O I P B X Z O N
U L T Q E M V W E H T T A M E
G A S N F A R T X F Z V A O V
H W I O E S U C I T I V E L E
I L R I D T W L Y A E V L O S
H E H T Q S M L A S P U E S Y
C V C A Y R H Q E W F N B F T
A L S L F I R S T J O H N O N
L E U E R T H U F R T Y G E
L A W S V H A I M E H E N N W
M T E E N I N Y T R I H T O T
D A J R H Y R E V E R H T S E
```

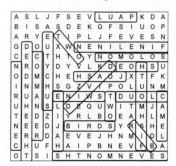

Puzzle 58

```
A S L J F S E V L U A P K D A
B I S A S D E K G F S I U O P
A R Y E T I P L J F E V E S N
G D O U X W N E N I L E N I F
C E C T H T O Y N O M O L O S
N R O Y D Y V L K D E O H S U
O D M C H E H S A O J X T F K
I N M H S G Z V P O L U N M
R U A U E N I W S T D U O L C
U H N S L D E Q U W I T M J A
T E D Z I Y R L B O E A H L M
N E E D J B I R D S Y R S H E
E R R D A E V E J H N W N I O L
C H U F H A I P B N E V A B A
O T S I S H T N O M E V E N E S
```

Puzzle 59

```
A B S O P N L E A H S I M K U
E L J S E F T L E A M H S I Q
N E H P E T S K Q U O L T N A
A B O B V B I A E E S D O G B
P E A L A M T U M O E X I S S
C Z R M S H P N A S S Z R A A
H E A O H H A O M V O W A U H
I J H L T A B M A V O N C L A
E M H P A I I E O D B N Y S E
H A X S E R H L X I M P I O I
A R N B Z A T O C H V R S N A
I O B A U Z N S I N S I Y T A
A B S U E A H C C A Z O D D A
S E L O P R O E H T Y C U S H
I D N M W E J H P E S O J Q U
```

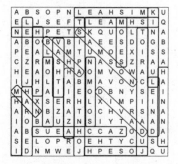

Puzzle 60

```
E R T A E N M D N A S U O H T
D W H Q N T Y H J O I B N S W
M L R P O Y Y T N E V E S E O
X N E Q N O M O L O S N B F D
C N E G K E V L E W T I R Y U
J O L T Y W X M Y T N E V E S
O X R W H J K L Y E N M A R Y
W T S E V E N I N T N E M O M
T W P L U T A D E G N A H C H
Y O U V X I H P V H N B H S L
T F X E N E R B E H C U R E X
R I X M B L I U S M K R T E H
I S E V A O L E V I F N U R V
H Y B A B Y L O N T R E H H
T A N E T G N I L K N I W T C
```

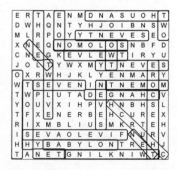

Puzzle 61

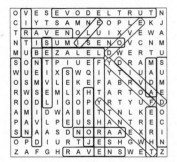

Puzzle 62

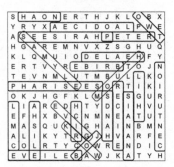

Puzzle 63

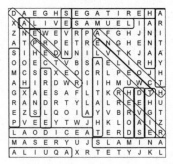

Puzzle 64

Puzzle 65

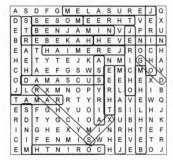

Puzzle 66

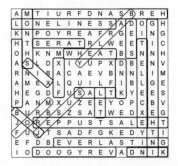

Puzzle 67

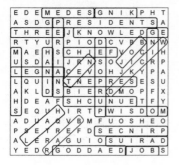

Puzzle 68

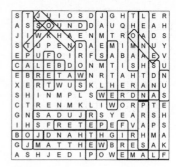

Puzzle 69

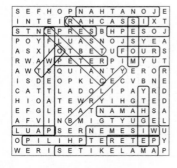

Puzzle 70

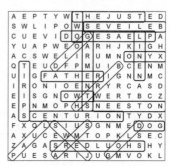

Puzzle 71

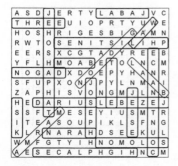

Puzzle 72

Puzzle 73

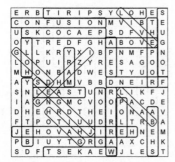

```
A W E W H C O N E B N E M K L
O P A A R O N L P O I Z U R E
S D F T C E R T H E Y N O A H
C T H E G A R D E N B O M M U
X C V R T I X S K R R K A Y
L J F I H A O N U B A B E H S
C A I N L S D F S T Y E D A R
L P O T I E U T I U R F E R H
W R T O E J B G U L V B Z B A
E F I W S N A C B A X I A Z
R V L I G H T E B Y T H H S A
D I T N Y B M Q U I Y R C T V
N O S E T I K E L A M A L I W
A X D R E T R N H Y R T E N M
P I U Q W E R U Y T P O M L K
```

Puzzle 74

```
A W R S E F T S R O T B E D B
O D L E I F E H T F O Y L I L
H R E H Y D N A L A S F H U O
S I I S M N E R E A D Y O D O
E H T U J A W O R D O F G O D
M T E R S H M N I N H O J O K
A D I L C T H Y K U P T L L E
J L F U V A B E V I L D E B C
E U D B Q N T A H T R A M O M
R F O L K O Y T R E D E B T S
E H O R T J A F V B I R E R Y
T T G U J S U C S A M A D E R
E I P A G R E E D L J U H T A
P A B R A H A M W E H T T A M
D F O Z X S E M I T L L A W E
```

Puzzle 75

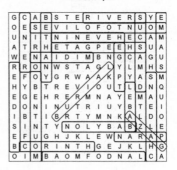

```
R A F H S I H S R A T G H P S
T H E G A R D E N O F E D E N
A Y T D E B A H A R O V A E A
B N A R F F W R E A Q L B F I
M M B S C P O O K J H E R I D
A O R I S Z A U G H E W A L R
D U A S I S E X R E S T H F A
A N H E U S J E Z T S W A O U
F T A N T E N R A G E O M E G
A C M E W L E R T J I E K E T
H A M G E T Q U I D B O N R H
A R T Y L S E R O I U S E T O
O M L I V I N G F O R E V E R
N E Y T E H R H G A D A R H N
A L M N O T X Y H T O M I T S
```

Puzzle 76

```
G C A B S T E R I V E R S Y E
O E S E V I L O F O T N U O M
U N I T N I N E V E H E C A M
A T R H E T A G P E E H S U A
W E N A I D I M B N G C A G U
R R O N W S T A G L Y L M H S
E F O Y G R W A A K P Y A S M
H Y B T R E V I O U T L D N Q
E G E H R E R M N A Y E M A U
D O N I N U T R I U Y B T E I
I B T I B R T Y M N K A L D O
S I N T Y N O L Y B A B Z L E
E F U G H J K L E W N A R A P
B C O R I N T H G E J K L H G
O I M B A O M F O D N A L C A
```

Puzzle 77

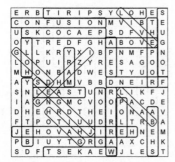

```
E R B T I R I P S Y L O H E S
C O N F U S I O N M V I B T E
U S K C O C A E P S D F V H U
O Y T R E D F G H A B O V E G
G L L K R Y X I B P N M F P N
L O P U I R Z Y R E S A G O O
M H O N B A D W E S T Y U O T
A Y S D H M V B B D N E I R F
S N L E A S T U N R L K F J
I A G N M C V O O P A C D E
D H E H R D T H E I O N A A V
F T P O T U U D R L T R B E M
J E H O V A H J I R E H N E M
P B I U Y T G R G A A X C H K
S D F T S E K A E W J L E S T
```

Puzzle 78

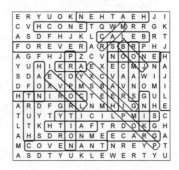

```
E R Y U O K N E H T A E H J I
C V H C O N E T Q W M R R G K
A S D F H J K L C A L E B R T
F O R E V E R A R S B R P H J
A G F H J P Z C V N O O N E H
Y U H I K R A E X E C M J N A
S D A E C O Y X C V A A W I J
D F O X V P M S B A V N O M I
H T N I R O C T E E R S G U L
A R D F G R L N M H G N H E
T U Y T Y T I C I L P M I S C
L T K H T I A F T R D O K G H
A H S D R O N M E C A R G B
M C O V E N A N T N R E Y P T
A S D T Y U K L E W E R T Y U
```

Puzzle 79

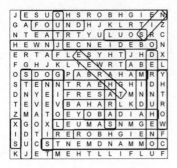

Puzzle 80

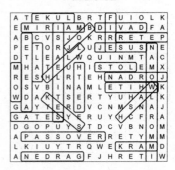

Puzzle 81

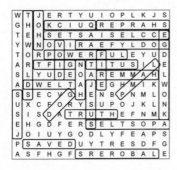

Puzzle 82

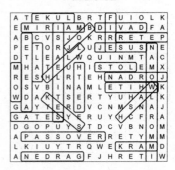

Puzzle 83

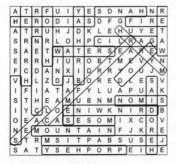

Puzzle 84

Puzzle 85

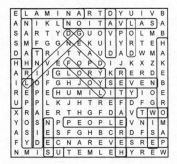

Puzzle 86

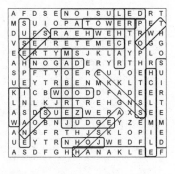

Puzzle 87

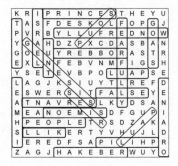

Puzzle 88

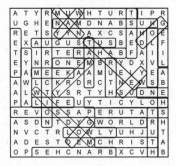

Puzzle 89

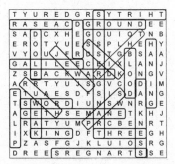

Puzzle 90

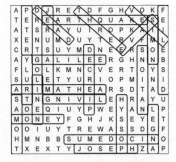

Puzzle 91

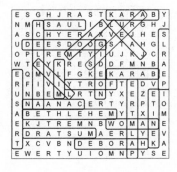

Puzzle 92

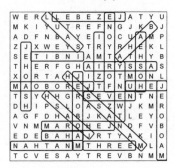

Puzzle 93

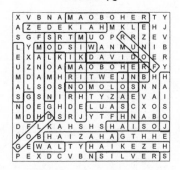

Puzzle 94

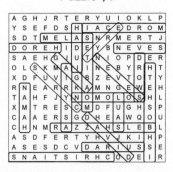

Puzzle 95

Puzzle 96

Puzzle 97

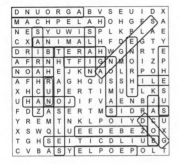

Puzzle 98

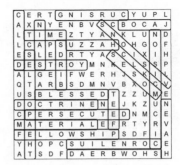

Puzzle 99

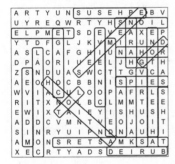

Puzzle 100

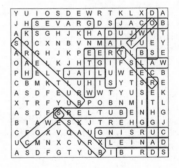

Puzzle 101

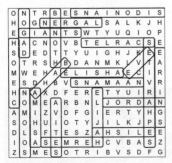

Go Deeper Into the Bible with These Resources

Layman's Bible Survey

Layman's Bible Survey explores the major periods of biblical history, showing how the different sections of scripture play a part in the grand scheme of God's Word. This fully illustrated reference includes twenty-four chapters that will take readers from "In the Beginning" to "John's Revelation of the Future."

Paperback / 978-1-63058-346-0 / $16.99

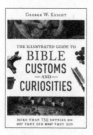

Illustrated Guide to Bible Customs and Curiosities

Why did people in the Bible wash each other's feet? What was wrong with Leah's "tender eyes"? What did Jesus mean about His "yoke" being "easy"? Readers will find answers to these questions and many more in *The Illustrated Guide to Bible Customs and Curiosities*. More than 750 clear, concise entries are included.

Paperback / 978-1-63058-468-9 / $7.99

The Student Bible Dictionary

Here's popular Bible reference for students of all ages—especially teens who seek to learn more about the Bible and its times. With more than 750,000 copies sold over the past 15 years, *The Student Bible Dictionary* has helped countless readers better understand scripture. Defining and explaining hundreds of Bible words, names, places, and concepts, this book has been expanded and updated with additional information from newer Bible translations.

Paperback / 978-1-63058-140-4 / $9.99